# ENGLISH DECORATIVE C

Art Nouveau to Art Deco

A concise guide to the most notable English potteries from 1875-1939.
**Individual Artists, Potters, Historical Background, Products, Marks, and References**

John Bartlett

Kevin Francis Publishing Ltd 1989
LONDON SE22 9JS
© copyright J Bartlett 1989

All rights reserved

## ABOUT THE AUTHOR

**John Bartlett is a graduate of the University of London and a Licentiate of Trinity College of Music.**

**His interest in ceramics began more than fifteen years ago, and the idea for this book came a few years later when he realised that many dealers and collectors had difficulity in readily obtaining information about ceramics of the art nouveau and art deco periods.**

**This book is thus the result of some twelve years of research by the author, who is today recognised by many as being a leading authority on English art pottery.**

# ACKNOWLEDGEMENTS

I am indebted to the many dealers, collectors, authors, museums, libraries and auction houses who have provided valuable information and allowed their pieces to be photographed.

I am also particularly indebted to the following collectors and specialists in decorative arts for their input: Janet Bonassera, Michael Bruce, John Edgeler, Shirley & Roger Edmundson, Peter Gooday, Malcolm Haslam, Michael John, Dan Klein, Pat & Charles Lancaster, Eva & Glyn White, Mary & Bernard Wright; and to the following museums and art galleries:-

Carisbrooke Castle Museum, Isle of Wight (Roy Brinton),
City Museum & Art Gallery, Stoke-on-Trent (Kathy Niblett),
Hampshire County Museum Service, Chilcomb House, Winchester (Margaret MacFarlane),
Ironbridge Gorge Museum (John Powell),
Maidstone Museums & Art Gallery (Henry Middleton)

Photography by John Bartlett with the exception of some plates and cover photo by Michael Bruce. Photographs marked 'HCMS' are of pieces owned by Hampshire County Museum Service.

**Design** *Francis Salmon*
**Artwork** *James Scannell*
**Word processing** *Simmone Standeven*
**Typesetting** *Microprint*
**Editorial** *Stephanie Bartlett*

# CONTENTS

**The names by which potters, wares and artists are commonly known are shown here. Refer to the index for additional names which do not appear in the contents.*

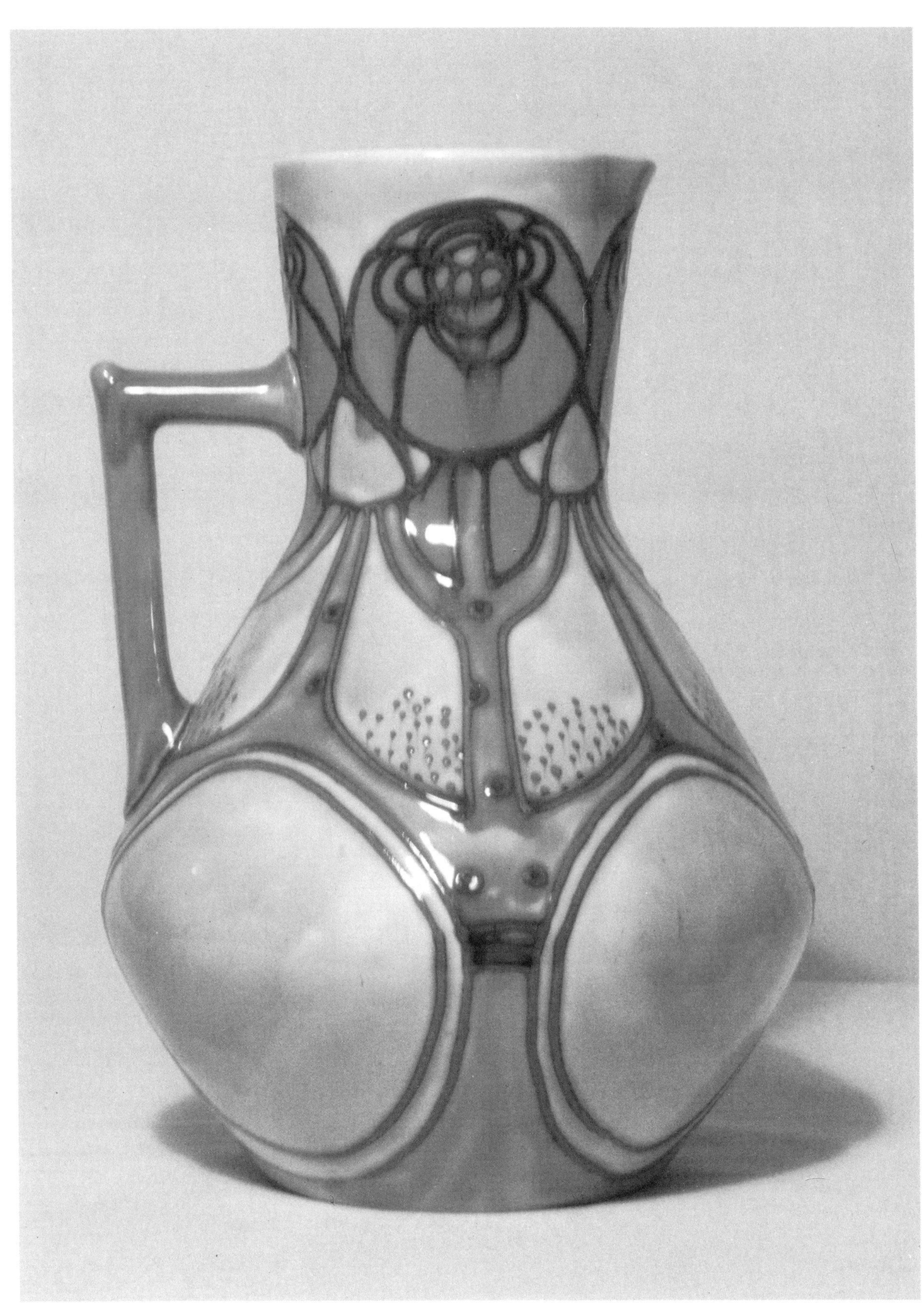

**Mintons**
*Jug, 288 mm high, in the 'Secessionist' style.*

**Burmantofts**

*Vase, 390 mm high, moulded with applique dragon chasing a dragonfly, marked 'Burmantoft's Faience', c.1881.*

# PREFACE

**The purpose of this book is to provide dealers and collectors of English decorative ceramics with a comprehensive guide to potteries and their products from approximately between the years 1875 and 1939, with particular attention to ornamental ceramics of the art nouveau and art deco styles.**

No survey of the English Potteries could ever be complete, and there are many widely collected products from potteries about which very little has been published. In recent years, though, particular interest in the art deco style has brought about a wealth of new publications on individual potteries, filling a much needed gap in our knowledge of products of this period. Interest also abounds in many minor potteries and studios (those of the West Country in particular), and new facts are regularly coming to light concerning these enterprises. Much research still needs to be done, however, and any gaps in this current volume are evident of that need.

Although the published bibliography of English Pottery is growing (almost trebling that of ten years ago) there are many dealers and collectors who need to be able to consult a single source of reference for the art nouveau to art deco period; and that is the primary aim of this present volume.

It is hoped that the comprehensive Bibliography in this book will direct the reader to further reference, and to this end a separate **Reference** section has been included under each pottery chapter. (In some cases this section is absent because of the lack of readily available material).

The References section also gives some indication of museums housing particular collections. Not all these collections are permanently displayed, however, so the reader should ascertain their availability before setting out to view.

Examples of many of the potteries described are included in the larger national collections, such as the City Museum and Art Gallery, Stoke-on-Trent, and the Victoria and Albert Museum, London. These national collections, because of their wide coverage, have only been referenced for specific potteries, and museums displaying small representative collections of English ceramics through the ages, such as the Holburne Museum, Bath, or the Curtis-Allen Gallery, Alton, have been similarly treated.

With few exceptions, the photographs in this book have been taken of pieces that were openly for sale in antiques shops, fairs or auctions. This gives a more realistic idea of the type of article that might be purchased, rather than by showing priceless museum pieces that may not only be atypical of a certain pottery but also out of reach of the general buyer.

The marks which are drawn or described are those most commonly associated with a particular pottery. They are not designed to be exhaustive but to give a general summary of what can be seen. There will always be deficiences and exceptions, and the reader should consult the **Bibliography** for any in-depth references required for a specific pottery.

An attempt has been made at categorising the pottery **production** and overall **quality**, based on quantities of output and average ceramic quality and decoration. Unfortunately, many potteries destroyed vital records of their production and styles, not thinking of any future need for such information, so only very poor estimates can be made of production in many cases.

The categories are only approximate and, naturally, views vary considerably as to what is good quality and what is poor quality.

An attempt has also been made at assessing the **availability** of pieces for the buyer. This category is more difficult to assess because of changing fashions and demand. For example, a particular type of ware suddenly becoming favourable may result in a sudden decrease in availability. Using all three categories together, however, may help to make an assesssment of demand and worth.

The categories are:-

| Production | Quality | Availability |
|---|---|---|
| Very Low | Poor | Rare |
| Low | Fair | Scarce |
| Moderate | Good | Uncommon |
| High | Very Good | Common |
| Very High | Excellent | Abundant |

The +/- symbol in the marks sections denotes the possible presence of a mark or feature.

***Doulton***
*Jug, 200 mm high, with incised marks 'BN' and 'Art Union of England', made at Lambeth, c.1900.*

# Introduction

**At first glance some pottery of the styles covered in this book may appear alien to the established period collector, but there is no doubt that the more important pieces exhibit an artistry without equal in any other art form.**

It was the realisation of this artistry less than thirty years ago that led to the collection and preservation of many ceramic creations that were previously dismissed as worthless. Now such creations are highly prized, and their collection is in part a reflection of the desire for items not mass-produced, i.e. studio works of quality, often unique and made by competent artists.

This desire was also present ninety years ago, at a time when the factory system of production was already well established in this country. The major potteries of the time realised the importance of studio work, and often operated craft sections which produced high quality pieces selling at competitive prices in specialist shops and, later, department stores such as Liberty and Selfridge. The craft work complemented the potteries' output of domestic ware for the lower-priced market. Indeed, the Poole Pottery today operates a similar balance of production.

The late Victorian era was in many ways a landmark in British pottery. Traditional shapes and decorations were giving way to new and sometimes extreme styles, the like of which had not been seen before, and might not be seen again.

Various styles started to evolve, the most spectacular of which was the *art nouveau* style which flourished in the late nineteenth century and which found expression in various art forms. For pottery, this style meant the chance to break away from the strictures of earlier designs and embark on a form that was to shake the foundations of traditionalism. The new style was well suited to the ceramic medium, adapting freely to the artistic expression of the period in shape, colour and function.

The wealth of output is amazing. It seems that every pottery in operation during the art nouveau period made some attempt at producing items in the new style. Doulton, with its vast output for domestic use, produced many fine art pieces, whilst smaller potteries such as Linthorpe catered almost exclusively for the manufacture of new art wares.

Studios at this time were important centres of experimentation, and their discoveries paved the way for modern ceramic development. The pottery and porcelain retailers, Howell & James of Regent Street, London, were responsible for promoting much amateur work, not only at their shop but also at regular exhibitions from 1876.

In design, art pottery was strongly influenced by the Arts and Crafts Movement, a body which included the designer William Morris, the illustrator Walter Crane, and painters Dante Gabriel Rosetti, Ford Madox Brown and Edward Burne-Jones among its members. These and other influences, such as the designer Christopher Dresser set the artistic trends of the day.

In 1888, the Arts and Crafts Exhibition Society was formed to display the work of artist craftsmen, and it encouraged the setting up of workshops which embodied its ideas and designs. Many designs portrayed a simplicity of form and decoration, whilst some were revivals of Gothic and Grecian shapes. The obsessions with fruit, flowers and "close to nature" designs and shapes were a particular aspect of the art nouveau style, and spread across most art forms.

A tendency towards medievalism was often shown through the work of Morris and Burne-Jones, and recurring themes such as the medieval galleon were very evident in media such as ceramics, metalwork, tapestries, stained-glass and enamel work. Certainly, these themes were taken up by potters such as William De Morgan and Harold Rathbone. When coupled with the Pre- Raphaelite ideas which still persisted, these created a particular style that proved popular until the First World War.

There was also a preoccupation with Orientalism, which continues to influence the minds of many artists and potters today. Japanese and Chinese designs were taken up by Christopher Dresser at Linthorpe, Charles Noke at Doulton, as well as by designers at Pilkington, the Ruskin Pottery and Bretby Art Pottery, to name but a few.

The Farnham Pottery copied medieval and Roman wares, and S E Collier at the Grovelands Potteries, Reading, produced *Silchester Ware* inspired by pottery excavated from the Romano- British town of Calleva Atrebatum (Silchester) nearby. This they freely did alongside the more mundane production of garden ornaments and chimney-pots!

The enormous variety of wares, however, needed an appreciative public, and various recreational organisations had grown up by the 1890's which, according to John Phillips, director of the Aller Vale Pottery, fostered...

*a greater enjoyment of life, from a growing appreciation and the use of the good things around us..... and a growing sympathy that is fostered by these societies between the cultured and refined mind and the uncultured.*

The President of one of these Societies, 'The Recreative Evening Schools', was Princess Louise, who included sculpture and other crafts amongst her own hobbies.

Country studios and potteries like Aller Vale flourished, and many, such as Compton in Surrey, took up the Arts and Crafts doctrines vigorously.

*The proper place for Arts and Crafts is in the country..... away from the complex, artificial, and often destructive influence of machines and the great town.*

So wrote Charles R Ashbee, a prominent member of the Arts & Crafts Exhibition Society, in his book 'Craftsmanship in Competitive Industry' (1908).

Yet, ironically, architects were using country craftsmanship in urban design, and potteries such as the Della Robbia Pottery regularly fulfilled ceramic commissions in several towns and cities.

The Edwardian era saw a tendency towards more classical shapes, and many studio potters found it difficult to sell their *new art* wares. Pilkington often sold their brilliant lustreware at less than the cost of production. A general slump in the industry just prior to the First World War did not help matters, and neither did the restrictions on the production of glazed pottery during the War or the loss of labour. Many potteries closed completely, never to reopen.

Ironically, a short-lived boost was given to the Staffordshire Potteries by the Royal Visit of King George and Queen Mary in 1913. This was reported as the first visit by a reigning monarch to the area since that of Edward II in 1323! Queen Mary became renowned as a collector of contemporary pottery, and regularly patronised Staffordshire concerns such as Moorcroft and Bernard Moore.

With the classical shapes came simplicity of form, and an early catalogue of the Poole Pottery exclaims,

*....the demand for simplicity, which is the keynote of present day furnishing, is combined with a more artistic perception of what is essential decoration. Profusion of ornamentation is now recognised as defeating its object, and in pottery the beauty of form, which is its chief attraction, must not be marred by a diversion of the eye from the symmetrical outline. The ornamentation should be just sufficient to emphasize the shape without detracting from its purity of line.*

After the First World War progress in ceramic chemistry brought about an increase in the number colours that were available for pottery. These new colours could withstand temperatures in excess of 1000 degrees centigrade in the kiln, thus allowing for greater variety. With increased colour, decoration became more profuse, bringing much admiration from a discerning public. Lustre wares were launched and re-launched. S Fielding & Co., for example, working with the Devon Pottery, Stoke, produced many colourful lustres on ornamental wares, although the majority of their output was decorative tableware.

Competition was rife, and rival showrooms at the pottery mecca of Holborn in London vied to satisfy the public's taste through the latest ceramic lines. New types of ware were proudly displayed, such as the floating-flower bowls and toilet sets which were all the rage in the early 1920's.

Annual exhibitions, such as the British Industries Fairs at Crystal Palace (and later Olympia) from 1915 to 1939, promoted high quality products through fierce competition. One-off exhibitions such as the British Industrial Art Exhibition at Knightsbridge during the summer of 1920, and various exhibitions abroad, such as at Paris in 1925, helped to place the pottery industry on an international footing. Indeed, the Ashtead Pottery (Ashtead, Surrey), which was set up to help ex-servicemen after the War, designed and modelled the *Wembley Lion* as a souvenir for the British Empire Exhibition at Wembley in 1924.

There was always a danger that art pottery would become too commercialised, and with the increase in moulded wares during the 1920's and 1930's, this almost became so. Wedgwood and other large pottery concerns were churning out mass-produced pieces, even though much work was done by hand. Many potteries thought it necessary to write "hand-painted" or similar legends on their articles in an attempt to deflect from their mass-production.

The larger potteries, besides mass-producing wares for the lower market, kept alive their craft sections. Wedgwood launched their successful *Fairyland Lustre*, and Doulton produced their *Sung* and *Chang* wares.

Wares were given individuality by being silver-mounted or having pewter attachments. An interesting trade developed for supplying wicker handles for teapots and other wares, from firms such as the Lichfield Basket & Cane Works, Hanley.

Tablewares became an increasingly important form of output for the larger potteries during the 1920's and 1930's, and a great variety of designs were executed. A detailed survey of these designs is beyond the scope of this book, but some of the more decorative ranges have been highlighted under the relevant chapters.

The importance of tablewares to The Potteries was brought home by C E Bullock's introductory address in 1935 to a lecture given by the artist Gordon Forsyth:

*When you come to discuss questions of art and design in pottery, bear in mind that, of the many millions of pounds' value of china and earthenware produced, probably 90% represents tableware. Therefore, really the most important design is not that which is included for purely decorative articles, but for articles that are used in connection with the service of food and drink.*

Gordon Forsyth's lecture concerned the Exhibition of Industrial Art at Burlington House, which was organised by the Royal Academy and the Royal

Society of Arts. He stressed the "educational importance of the appreciation of beauty in mass-produced articles" and the need to break down "the barriers between the fine arts and industrial arts".

Whether the art deco style was able to accomplish this is difficult to say. Certainly, several renowned artists attempted to design quality wares which could be produced cheaply, and the Harrods Tableware Exhibition of 1934 included many examples by designers such as Clarice Cliff, Charlotte Rhead and Susie Cooper.

Joseph Bourne & Son at Denby produced what they described as 'industrially produced Studio wares' from about 1930 to 1940. A good example of these is their *Danesby* range of ornamental items, popular with collectors today. The Pearl Pottery Company (PP & Co.) produced their *Cranston* range similarly, though these pieces were designed to complement their art deco fireplaces. 'Good clean lines' was an advertising slogan for much domestic and functional pottery of the later 1930's, and T G Green's *Cornish Kitchen Ware*, with its wide blue concentric bands on a white ground, exemplified the tenet for 'cleanliness in the modern home'.

Meanwhile, the real studio potters were taking a different approach. The 'back to first principles' movement was clearing the way to a very different style that would survive the next war. A revival of more traditional pottery was slowly beginning to emerge, and the continued interest in Chinese and Japanese traditional wares was extended in many cases to understanding the basis of their production rather than by simply copying their decoration. Bernard Leach, for example, went to Japan to learn, and his pupils learned from him.

Charles Vyse, who had been making slip-moulded figurines at Chelsea during the 1920's, concentrated on stonewares from the early 1930's, and his later stoneware creations (c. 1936-1938) were strongly influenced by Oriental styles. The sculptor/potter Reginald Wells was also producing stonewares at his pottery in Storrington, Sussex (c. 1924 to 1940), which he regularly marked *SOON*.

The solid earthy appearance with minimal surface decoration on studio wares at this time was also promoted by William Staite- Murray (1881-1962), who, having also experimented with Japanese stoneware styles during the early 1920's, went on to create pieces in the late 1930's which were influenced by medieval English earthenware. Michael Cardew, a pupil of Bernard Leach, also concentrated on slip-decorated earthenware in the English tradition from 1926 at his pottery in Winchcombe, Gloucestershire. In 1941, he left for West Africa where he taught and later made pottery using local materials.

Two world wars certainly took their toll on the manufacture of decorative ceramics, but their ability to survive is much to do with a discerning public's desire for quality products. The equivalent desire for hand-thrown and hand-decorated pieces by craftsmen rather than by machine or production line has ensured a future for tradional art pottery, and there are pieces being produced today which will take their place alongside such historical landmarks as Doulton's flambe or De Morgan's *Persian Colours*.

Certainly the popularity of ceramics amongst collectors is increasing, and wares produced during the period covered by this book are beginning to acquire a well-deserved place amongst the most precious of antiques. Anyone who has ever tried to learn the art of pottery throwing will appreciate the skill and artistry involved - a skill which Chaucer sums up admirably in his verse: "The lyf so short, the craft so longe to learne".

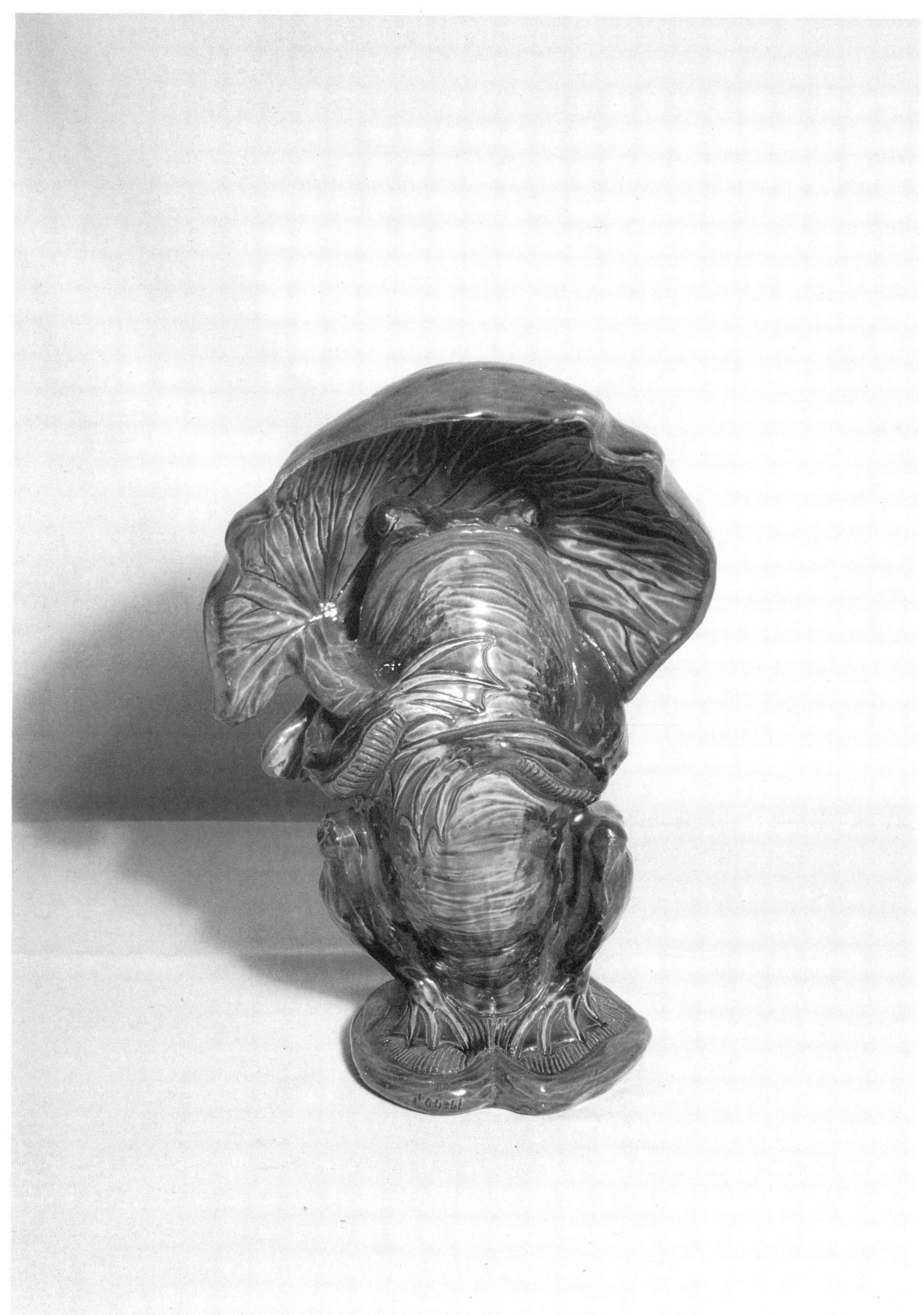

**_Brannam_**
_Model of a frog with lily leaf umbrella, 300 mm high, marked 'C.H.brannam, Barum, 1901'._

# The Identification of Wares

**Not all pottery is marked, but although the absence of a mark can cause difficulty in identification and therefore authentication of a piece there are other pointers which may reveal the identity of the factory. Comparisons of style, shape and glaze can often be made to positively identify a piece, since many potteries were remarkably consistent in their output.**

Dating is more difficult, but even without a date mark there are other indicators which can provide good estimates. After 1891 all wares for export from this country were required to be marked 'England', and from the 1920's to the present time the mark 'Made in England' is common-place. These and other pointers are useful in placing pieces in context, and many of the individual potteries utilised their own slogans which can be helpful in dating their wares.

During the period covered by this book various methods of marking were in operation. In general it is possible to recognise five basic types of mark: a **factory mark**, an **artist's / decorator's mark**, a **pattern number** and a **date mark**. Each of the marks may occur independently or in various combinations. It is also possible that the factory mark, artist and thrower are one and the same person, so care must be taken when using marks for identification.

Naturally, the collector desires the appearance of as many marks as possible, and several potteries in this book were particularly consistent in their marking. An example from a piece of Pilkington Lapis Ware exhibits the following marks:-

**i) the Pilkington factory mark: Royal Lancastrian**
**ii) the incised initials 'ETR' for Edward Thomas Radford, the thrower**
**iii) the incised pattern number '157'**
**iv) the painted underglaze monogram 'R' for Gwladys Rodgers, the artist**
**v) the date '1928'**
**vi) the stamp 'Made in England'**

The **factory** mark is the mark most commonly found. It may contain the complete name of the pottery or the title of its ware (eg 'Carlton Ware'). It can sometimes be abbreviated (as 'P' for Pilkington) or occur as a picture or monogram (as the ship for Della Robbia Pottery or the 'TTC' monogram for Torquay Terra-Cotta Co.)

The mark may be stamped or incised in the wet clay, painted or stamped in paint underglaze, transfer-printed or painted overglaze. Sometimes the same mark may be executed in a variety of ways. Few potteries were totally consistent with their factory marks, and most changed their styles of marking to suit their output over the years. It is rare that one can date a piece precisely using the factory mark alone, but it is often possible to date to within ten years.

The **artist's** or **decorator's mark** in addition to the factory mark is often taken as a sign that a piece was not mass-produced, but common sense must weigh the balance between the piece under scrutiny and the production habits of the factory. Artists were justly proud of their work, and it was common practice at large studios to encourage artists to be inventive with their designs. At Doulton, where a large number of artists were employed, we are fortunate to have detailed lists of artist marks as a means of identification.

The artist's mark is more often to be found painted underglaze. This really is a reflection of the process involved during the creation of a piece, in that decoration would usually occur after the first (or biscuit) firing. The artist would usually sign his or her initials in one of the colours used in the decoration, though for many years underglaze blue seems to have been an unwritten standard marking colour in England and Europe.

The artist's mark need not necessarily occur on the base of a piece. Arthur Eaton at Doulton's regularly signed his name within the body of the decoration; and on the black and red landscape flambes it is worth looking for the occurrence of his signature - so many people miss it!

The presence of a **thrower's mark** is greatly valued by the collector, since this generally guarantees the individuality of a piece, particularly if the mark is hand-written. It is also a mark which is relatively rare on non-studio wares.

At the Martin Brothers' studio for example, Walter Martin was the principal thrower and signed his work accordingly. At Linthorpe, Henry Tooth undertook much of the throwing, but his mark frequently consists of his initials stamped in the clay, and is no guarantee that he personally made a particular piece. The large number of pieces available without his stamp, however, and the relatively short life of the pottery tend to indicate that he had some involvement in all of the pieces so stamped.

At some studios (Elton and Leach, for example), the thrower was also the decorator and owner of the establishment. In these cases there would naturally be only one mark used to indicate all three occupations. The addition of a separate **designer's mark** is not common. It is closely linked to the thrower's mark since the designer would indicate to the thrower the style of a piece. At Linthorpe, Christopher Dresser's signature was used on pieces made to his design, and often resides with the thrower's mark.

A mark which can give an indication of style, shape

or colour is the **pattern number**. Researchers have spent long hours trying to interpret the pattern numbers used by different potteries, with considerable success, and we are much indebted to their labours in this.

It is easy to be misled by the various codes and scratchings that appear with annoying regularity on pieces, since many factories kept no proper records of their markings, and so their true nature may never be uncovered. To be certain of a pattern number, reference should always be made to the habits of the factory in question. At Poole, for example, a code of 10R indicated a pattern of geometric lines. A code of 0R, however, indicated the same pattern style, but with the geometric lines further apart. This code was purely an indication of decoration, and gave no guide to shape.

Generally, codes' that indicated shape are to be found incised on a piece under the glaze, and would be marked by the thrower. Decoration codes are more often to be found painted on, over or under the glaze.

At some potteries the number codes might refer to the quantity of pieces made, whilst at others they might refer to catalogue entries. At Brannam, pieces could be ordered by shape from their catalogue, and decorated to the customer's choice of colour.

In addition to the above marks there may be a **date mark**. At the Pilkington Pottery, Roman numerals were used at some stage to indicate the year of production (eg 'XI' for 1911), whilst the Martin Brothers incised both the year and the month on their wares ('7-1889' as July, 1889, for example). At Wedgwood a complicated method of date registration was used at one time to mark their pottery and glass products, but the codes can be readily interpreted, and reveal much about a particular piece.

Some potteries dated their pieces infrequently. At the Moorcroft Pottery, for example, the presence of a date is rare, it usually occurring only during the first few years of production at the Cobridge works (1913 -1915 approx.).

The collector will doubtless come across types of marks other than those described above. Becoming familiar with the range of wares from a pottery is as equally important as knowing the main marks.

Reproductions can be a nuisance to the collector of originals, even though they may be reproduced in good faith and be of good quality. Usually one can tell from the mark and from a certain freshness of style whether a piece is a reproduction. Doulton have reproduced their flambe styles of the 1920's using a similar mark, and the later Walter Moorcroft styles and marks are similar to (but to the trained eye discernible from) those of William Moorcroft.

A good line is well worth repeating, and will often maintain a pottery business. The immensely popular Meissen porcelain figurines have been continually produced and reproduced all over Europe. Similarly the current fashion for Victorian jardineres has created a market for reproductions, particularly as the originals are fetching high prices and becoming difficult to acquire.

When examing marks the collector should always beware of forgeries or restorations. A mark incised under the glaze would generally leave a burred edge where the displaced wet clay has been fired and then glazed. The displacement would be much less on pieces stamped under the glaze. Collectors should be wary of incised marks without any displacement, which have been scratched into the finished piece at a later date.

The lack of a mark and a smooth unglazed base could indicate that grinding has taken place, something which is undertaken to eliminate basal chips, and which is more common on glass than on pottery pieces. At the pottery, grinding is usually undertaken using carborundum stone to smooth down sharp edges of glaze. The collector should be suspicious, however, of any clean scratch-free bases which might indicate that grinding has taken place after leaving the factory.

Kiln marks are often present on the base of pieces, and with some potteries they were almost a trademark. For example, most Elton pieces display three equally placed, raised, round marks which were left by the kiln supports when firing the glaze.

## General Characteristics of Wares

The form or feel of a piece is as much an aid to identification as the mark. Pieces may be heavy or light, thinly or thickly potted, thrown on the wheel, moulded, modelled or coiled. Pottery can exhibit many characteristics.

Pots which are hand thrown will often not have completely smooth interiors, such that the collector should be able to feel the ribbing inside a piece where the thrower has 'brought up' the pot on the wheel. Mass-produced pieces will invariably have smooth interiors, and moulded wares will bear one or more straight mould lines revealing the edges of contact of the mould. Moulded pieces are also generally much lighter in weight than hand-thrown pieces of similar size.

Pieces may exhibit a variety of glazes, quite apart from the variety of clays used to form the pottery body. Some glazes will be high (ie of a high gloss), others matt or even crystalline. Many potteries experimented with flambes and other reducing glazes, created at very high temperatures in the kiln. Doulton's flambes and Ruskin's 'high-fired' glazes are much prized by collectors, not only for their impressive colours but also for their comparative rarity. Lustre glazes are similarly prized.

Some wares were created as stoneware, some as earthenware and others as terra-cotta or porcelain.

The pottery body is a useful additional aid to identification, and may frequently be revealed at the base of a piece.

## Pottery Styles

Another aid to identification is the style of a piece. Firstly there is the **shape**. The Oriental influence was strong during the latter half of the 19th century, and consequently this is reflected in vases with bulbous bases and tapered cylindrical necks. The Ruskin Pottery in particular promoted these shapes, and continued the style through to the Edwardian era.

Bulbous shapes were a natural extension to the graceful curvilinear styles of the Victorian period, though the earlier styles persisted. The Ault Pottery continued to produce Victorian classical pieces into the 1920's. Their jardinieres are heavy in design and exhibit the characteristic Victorian penchant for frills and scroll-work on their boat-like or deep tulip-shaped bowls.

The Victorian zest for classical Greek scenes and Attic shapes was well catered for by the Potteries. Mintons' pâte-sur-pâte wares were noble exponents of this art form, as were the impressive enamel wares of the Watcombe Pottery. The *Grecian urn* was a favourite model for the Wedgwood factory, whilst the Ault Pottery used the outline of a Grecian vase as part of their factory mark for many years.

The Pre-Raphaelite influence was also strong during the Victorian era and we have been left many fine examples of painted wares as a result. Flat-faced plates which could easily be painted were produced alongside plaques and tiles, and skilled artists at Studios such as Minton's in South Kensington and Doulton's in Lambeth created the familiar portraits and scenes that artists such as Rosetti and Burne-Jones made famous.

By contrast there were also exponents of the avant-garde during this period. The designer Dr Christopher Dresser broke away from the traditional style of pottery, and after the publication of his volume 'Studies in Design' (1875) began to put his ideas into practice at potteries such as Linthorpe and Ault. His shapes were less bulbous but equally simple, relying on the use of angles and modelling for effect. His curious South American designs appealed to the Victorian taste for the unusual, but his streaky glazes and patterns were not so well received.

Dresser's designs did much to change the way of thinking concerning pottery style, and in many cases he was original. Individualism was an increasing trend during the late 19th century and seemed to exist quite happily alonside Morris's medievalism and the oriental and near-eastern influences.

De Morgan produced vases in the Persian style, and the Aller Vale Pottery tried to emulate Moorish styles. At Linthorpe, Dresser produced some Japanese style tea-wares, the shapes of which were later to be the simple foundations for decoration in reduced glazes by such exponents as Bernard Moore. The Bretby Pottery openly declared their Chinese and Japanese influences in named wares such as *Carved Bamboo Ware*, whilst Maw & Co. emulated Middle-Eastern designs in their large stoneware vases with ear-like handles.

The Della Robbia Pottery existed solely to produce pieces in the style of the 15th century Italian Renaissance, and some unusual gourd-shaped bottles and vases emerged from the Burmantofts Pottery strongly imitating primitive African wares.

Such was the range of international influences in English pottery - influences which had been spurred on by the Great Exhibition of 1851.

Europe, however, was not without its own particular style, and from the late 1870's the art nouveau style took the pottery world by storm. Weird shapes emerged and pieces became suddenly asymmetrical. Handles twisted over the necks of vases (compare Elton and Brannam), and shapes were often florally inspired, with extensive external modelling.

Grotesques, whether derived on purpose or by accident through misshapen pieces, became popular, and the Martin Brothers found a new market for their stylised birds with human heads, as did Brannam with his devil jugs and other monsters.

During the 1920's there was a more general trend towards angular forms, assisted by an increase in moulded wares. Bowls were produced with square and hexagonal sides, and towards the end of the decade more avant-garde shapes were being designed by Clarice Cliff. Models of contemporary subjects appeared, such as motor- cars and planes, which doubled as tea-pots or salt-cellars, and an interesting assortment of artistically influenced shapes were created, such as Louis Wain's model cats in the Cubist style.

In looking at shape, therefore, it is possible to generalise on trends from the middle of the 19th century through to the middle of the 20th century on style alone, viz:-

| | |
|---|---|
| **1860-1875** | **Traditional English pottery as exemplified by Doulton's of Lambeth. Rounded jugs, vases and bowls. Victorian classicism.** |
| **1875-1910** | **The age of art nouveau. More bulbous shapes. Strong international influences.** |
| **1910-1939** | **More angularity, less bulbous forms. A return to less complex shapes. The age of art deco.** |

It is generally much easier to identify wares by means of **decoration** rather than by shape, since many potters obtained their individuality through the former characteristic.

We can, however, recognise certain decorative styles which have been in part a response to public demand and taste in any one period. Doulton's output prior to 1875, for example, was fairly dull decoratively, but after this date brighter colours were more in evidence as a response to brighter decoration in the home.

Technical achievements in ceramics which extended the range of colours available also assisted in the creation of this brighter aspect. Experiments in glazes were a continuing occupation of potteries in the search for new and rival finishes, such that a large range of reducing glazes was produced through to the 1920's; but not all potteries were able to promote this development, as the technology was complex and the equipment costly and specialised.

The following list, though not exhaustive, gives an indication of the extensive involvement of potteries in producing glazes by reduction:

| | |
|---|---|
| **Doulton's** | *:flambés, crystaline and sang-de-bouf glazes.* |
| **Linthorpe** | *:some reduced glazes of poorish quality* |
| **Maw & Co** | *:lustres, similar to De Morgan's* |
| **Moorcroft** | *:rouge flambés, celadons: all with high glazes* |
| **Bernard Moore** | *:rouge flambés: mainly monochrome with a high glaze* |
| **W. De Morgan** | *: lustres: generally matt or silky finish* |
| **Pilkingtons** | *:lustres: mirror and glass-like effects* |
| **Poole** | *::some early monochrome lustres (c.1904-1919)* |
| **Ruskin** | *:reducing colours, rouge flambés, viridian flambes,semi-lustres, "souffle" and crystaline glazes* |
| **A.J. Wilkinson** | *:lustres on porcelain, rouge flambé* |
| **Wedgwood** | *:lustres on porcelain: highly decorative* |

Trends in decoration are often reflected in the development of the potteries themselves. At Moorcroft the changes in decorative style are very evident, and one can easily see the difference between the style of pieces produced prior to 1913 and those produced after, with another change occurring about 1930.

There are also artists and studios associated with one particular period of decoration, such as Clarice Cliff or Charlotte Rhead. Their creations in the art deco style consisted of bright decorative lines emphasising simple but impressive shapes. Dramatic colour combinations are evident, such as yellow and black; orange, yellow and blue; and orange and green. The simplified floral motifs and abstract geometrical patterns ensure that the art deco style is easily identifiable and not difficult to discern from its more sophisticated counterpart, the art nouveau style.

The motifs used for decoration by potteries throughout the period covered by this book have been generally consistent - only the styles have changed. Floral patterns, for example, have always been popular, whether executed by painting and enamelling (as at Doulton) or by sgraffito work (as by the Martin Brothers) or by modelling (as by Elton).

The more classical pieces of the late Victorain period utilised foliage as a means of background decoration, emerging in its own right within the art nouveau style. Fruit, flowers and vegetable designs were typical forms of decoration on art nouveau pieces, the patterns often extending to the outside of pieces as modelling in relief. Art nouveau flowers, however, were often depicted with the stem and roots of the plant as well!

The Arts and Crafts followers also utilised forms of foliage in their designs, and frequently used acorns and leaves as backgrounds for such subjects as leaping deer or exotic birds. Doulton's novel method of impressing real leaves into the wet clay and then colouring the impressions was an extension of the foliage motif.

Recurring decorative themes were common, such as the galleon (as utilised by William De Morgan, Walter Crane at Maw & Co., and William Mycock at Pilkington) or the *Liberty Cats* (as at Brannam, Baron and Aller Vale) or *Liberty Owl* (as at Farnham, Brannam, Denby's *Danesby ware* or by Elton). Also, Pilkington and Doulton seem at one time to have been fascinated by a particular species of fish, the 'John Dory'!

It is not easy, however, to generalise about decorative motifs. There will always be individual designs associated with one particular artist or pottery, such as Gordon Forsyth's heraldry or Daisy Mackeig-Jones' fairies. The collector needs to use decoration not as a sole means of identification but in conjunction with shape, style and marks. Artists did move from factory to factory, and factories were clever at imitating each other's styles, especially for the lower-priced market.

Hancock & Sons' *Morris Ware*, for example, which was designed by George Cartlidge, was similar to some of Moorcroft's designs, and Pilkington's popular lustres were sometimes emulated by potteries such as C. T. Maling & Sons Ltd. of Newcastle-on Tyne during the 1930's, and by S. Fielding & Co. even earlier. Fielding also produced leaf-shaped bowls and plates during the later 1920's and early 1930's similar to Carlton Ware.

The joy of looking at pottery is in its infinite variety, and there will always be similarities as well as surprises.

# ALLER VALE ART POTTERY

## Newton Abbot, Devon (1881-1924)

### Typical Wares: Terra-cotta

### Historical Background

**The Aller Vale Pottery was established as the Aller Pottery in 1865, producing initially brown bodied earthenware for domestic use. In 1881, after the original pottery was damaged in a fire, John Phillips set up the Aller Vale Art Pottery, recruiting workers from the Newton Abbot School of Art which he helped to found ten years previously.**

Phillips was particularly interested in the principles of the Arts & Crafts Movement, and encouraged the local community by running art and craft classes. The Torquay Terra-Cotta Company and Watcombe Pottery were already established and may have influenced Phillips in his enterprise. At Aller Vale, Phillips ensured that pieces were hand-made in the traditional way using locally obtained materials.

In 1886, Phillips took on an apprentice by the name of Charles Collard, who later went on to found the Honiton Pottery and the Crown Dorset Pottery at Poole.

In 1890, national attention was drawn to the pottery when Princess Louise opened the fourth annual exhibition of the Kingskerswell Cottage Art Schools, Torquay; and it is recorded that in the 1890's some pieces sold at Liberty's.3

Phillips died in 1897, and the business was taken over by Hexter, Humpherson & Co. who also later purchased the Watcombe Pottery.

In 1901, the Aller Vale Pottery merged with the Watcombe Pottery at Torquay to form the Royal Aller Vale & Watcombe Pottery Company. The works at Aller Vale closed in 1924, much of the labour force having already moved to other local potteries.

### Products

The early styles are crude and unglazed, the pieces being seldom marked; but from 1887, there was a noticeable change of style and the wares became heavily glazed and well marked, exhibiting floral and insect designs in thickly coloured slips. These were in the manner of the French *barbotine* style, and were mainly vases with decoration in bright colours on a blue, yellow, green or red-brown ground.

A common characteristic of the barbotine pieces is the occurrence of the painted flower motif on only one side of the vase, the reverse usually depicting a simple complementary leaf pattern, such as a bullrush.

A pattern based on Isnik Pottery and known as *Persian* was produced from about 1885, and is characterised by blue tulips and other flowers such as hyacinths and carnations.

A strong influence on design at Aller Vale was an Italian artist named Marcucci, who created Italianate scroll patterns from about 1890. His name is sometimes to be found on pieces of his design incised or painted within the decoration.

Some of the wares were given specific titles, such as *Sandringham*, *Abbotskerswell* and *Crocus*. The latter ware consisted of an art nouveau crocus design, usually on tall-necked vases, and includes the stem, bulb and leaves of the crocus as well as the flower, in green and white on a deep blue background.

*Sandringham* featured a blue scroll pattern on a white ground, and was named by the Princess of Wales who purchased several pieces. *Abbotskerswell* was a simple daisy pattern. Other patterns included *Scandy* and *Rhodian* (both reminiscent of Prince of Wales feathers) and various forms of cockerel design.

Generally, the floral motif was a favourite means of decoration on Aller Vale pieces, the surface decoration being

*Selection of 'barbotine' wares.*

plentiful and the colours bright. The deep red body of the ware was a suitable background for the designs and types of glaze employed.

Designs often emulated old Moorish and Mediterranean ceramic styles, and, although the majority of output was in terracotta, some pieces were created in white clay (particularly the *Sandringham* pattern) or a mixture of red and white.

A ware known as *Daison* was advertised in 1913, and consisted of painting on a matt ground.

A great deal of ware was made for the souvenir trade, and many pieces contained popular mottoes, although it is believed that only one person was employed to etch the mottoes at any one period. Designs after the merger with Watcombe included more and more souvenir wares, such as cottages and windmills, many of which were of low quality.

The collector should note that potteries in the Torquay area often produced similar designs,and recurring themes were common across the Devon Potteries generally. The Longpark Pottery, for example, working from 1905 to 1957, produced a popular decoration of yellow daffodils on a bright green ground, the whole bearing a high gloss glaze. This design was reproduced at Aller Vale and elsewhere. Collectors will frequently find styles imitated at Aller Vale from a wide range of potteries, Linthorpe, Burmantofts and Brannam being just a few examples.

**References**

*1) 'The Old Torquay Potteries' by D & E Lloyd Thomas, pub. Stockwell, 1978.*

*2) 'Collard, the Honiton & Dorset Potter' by Carol & Chris Cashmore; pub. privately, 1983. (Includes detail of pattern codes)*

*3) 'Torquay Pottery 1870-1940'; catalogue of an Exhibition at Bearne's and Bonham's, London, August, 1986; pub. Torquay Pottery & Collectors' Society.*

*4) 'Ceramics for Gentlemen of Taste: the Torquay Potteries & Their Products'; article by Carol Cashmore in the Antique Dealer & Collector, August, 1986.*

| Type of Ware | Production | Quality | Availability |
|---|---|---|---|
| Early wares | Low | Poor | Uncommon |
| Post-1887 wares | Moderate to High | Good to Very Good | Uncommon (grotesques: Scarce) |

**Marks**

| | | |
|---|---|---|
| Incised: | Phillips<br>Aller | c.1881-1887 |
| | Phillips<br>Newton Abbot | c.1881-1887 |
| Impressed | ALLER VALE | 1887-1901 |

(early pieces often occur without a factory mark, but occasionally bear a small impressed 'T', Maltese Cross or crescent shape; other marks have also been noted)

| | | |
|---|---|---|
| | ALLER<br>VALE<br>DEVON<br>ENGLAND | c.1891-1918 |

± H.H. & Co. (after 1897)

| | | |
|---|---|---|
| Painted: | Aller Vale<br>England | c.1891-c.1901 |

(NB: 'Royal Aller Vale' refers to the merger with Watcombe, i.e. post-1901)

± pattern numbers (A to Z with numerals, indicating variety (usually the colour of the background, eg C2)

± decorator's mark

There is no record of pieces being dated, except as commemoratives where the date sometimes appears as part of the decoration, but never on the base. Early pieces tend to have an unglazed base.

# The Ashby Potters' Guild

## Woodville, Derbyshire (1909-1922)

Typical Wares: earthenware, lustres, flambé

### Historical Background & Products

**The Ashby Potters' Guild was a studio pottery established by Pascoe Tunnicliffe in 1909. The pottery specialised in glaze effects, and often used multicoloured glazes over a red clay body.**

Some fine blue and ruby lustres were produced, together with crystalline glazes (also often in blue) and a rouge flambe. The Pottery Gazette records that a specimen of the pottery's crystalline glaze was sold to the Copenhagen Museum in 1913.

Some vases of good quality were produced during the early 1920's of varying sizes, together with floating-flower bowls, pot-pourri and ginger jars, plaques, covered vases, tobacco and biscuit jars, cake-stands and ink-stands. Many designs were orientally inspired. Some miniature pieces were also produced, and many of these were created using a white clay body.

Pieces were exhibited at the Ghent Exhibition in 1913 and the British Industrial Arts Exhibition in April, 1920. This latter exhibition included the Guild's *Vasco* art pottery, the manufacture of which had been temporarily suspended during the Great War. Vasco art pottery consisted of decoration in variegated crystalline and lustre glazes, and also enamel colours. At the exhibition an orange flambé glaze also attracted attention.

Besides the glaze effects, decorative styles included floreate designs, such as arrangements of oak leaves, and many were quite individual in character.

In 1922, the pottery merged with William Ault's Pottery to form the partnership 'Ault and Tunnicliffe' (ref. Ault).

Ashby Guild pieces are not widely collected, owing to the scarcity of items available. The quality, however, is good and the glaze effects are attractive. Unfortunately little is known about the many ranges of ware produced by this pottery.

*Vase, 135 mm high, lustre glaze, marked 'AB' in monogram.*

| Type of Ware | Production | Quality | Availability |
|---|---|---|---|
| All wares | Low to Moderate | Good to Very Good | Scarce |

**Marks**

| | | | |
|---|---|---|---|
| Printed or impressed: | ASHBY GUILD | (within oval) | 1909-1922 |

# ASHTEAD POTTERS LTD 1923-1935

## Victoria Works Ashtead, Surrey

Typical Wares: earthenwares

## Historical Background

**The Ashtead Pottery was founded in 1923 by Sir Lawrence Weaver, a civil servant, who as vice chairman of the Rural Industries Bureau wanted to establish new careers for disabled ex-servicemen.**

A fund was set up through a committee headed by Sir Lawrence Weaver's wife, Kathleen, which included Sir Bertram Clough Williams-Ellis, Stafford Cripps and the Reverend Edward Dorling among its members. Initial capital was provided by the British Red Cross Society and the Order of St. John and Jerusalem.

A small factory was obtained in Ashtead, and wares were marketed as Ashtead Potters Ltd. Lady Weaver became responsible for the welfare of the employees, whilst her husband actively marketed the pottery's products at every opportunity.

The first of these opportunities came in 1924, when Sir Lawrence Weaver was appointed Director of the UK section of the British Empire Exhibition, Wembley. He ensured that the Ashtead Potters were given ample press coverage; and the Duke and Duchess of York visited the Ashtead stand at the exhibition.

In 1928, the Duke and Duchess visited the pottery and were presented with a gift for their daughter, Elizabeth, of a "Christopher Robin" nursery set, which was subsequently issued as a numbered limited edition. The set was decorated from designs by E H Shepard, which were transfer-printed in black onto a white background and then handpainted.

Apparently Sir Lawrence Weaver was a great persuader, and many well-known artists gave their time to teach at the pottery or contributed their designs. Prominent amongst these was Phoebe Stabler, who designed extensively for the Poole Pottery, and who designed some striking figure models for Ashtead. Another prominent modeller at Ashtead was Percy metcalfe, and it was he who produced the design for the well- known 'Wembley Lion', which became the official souvenir of the 1924 Wembley Exhibition. The 'Lion' appeared subsequently in many forms, but as a simple moulded piece became an instant success.

At the height of its operation the pottery employed some forty workers, who produced a variety of shapes and designs. Many designs were copied from pieces in museums (such as the V & A) or from other samples of pottery at home and abroad. Lady Weaver is known to have given the name to the 'Brittany' shape of jug, for example, following a holiday in France.

The bulk of the pottery's output was tableware, and several commissions were fulfilled for specialist products, such as the honey-pot for Australian honey or the ceramic chocolate box for Carson's chocolates.

Sir Lawrence Weaver's death in 1930, coupled with the general depression in trade, heralded the end of the enterprise, and in 1935 the factory closed.

### Products

Mostly tableware was produced, such as dinner, tea, coffee and breakfast sets. Several small items were produced, which were also of a domestic nature, such as egg-cups, cruet sets and ashtrays (most interesting of which were the "CHO-KR Patent Extinguishing Ashtrays").

Amongst the larger items were electric lamp-bases and vases, though the largest pieces produced seem to have been no more than 490mm in height.

Most pieces were moulded, and were subsequently light in weight. Pieces heavier in weight were generally hand-thrown. Some pieces were modelled, such as figurines or the "Wembley Lions", and were produced by such artists as Phoebe Stabler, Percy Metcalfe, Allen G. Wyon and Donald Gibson.

Surface decoration was noticeably minimal, but where it occurred it was usually accomplished by hand-painted scenes (cottages in landscapes, for example) or painted transfer-prints (such

*Selection of decorated wares (courtesy of Leatherhead Museum). 1 to r:- i) small dish, 105 mm diam., painted underglaze, marked 'S5'. ii) pepper pot, 85 mm high, painted underglaze, not marked. iii) frog mustard pot (marked 'M19') and owl pepper pot (marked 'M20'), 95 mm high, painted underglaze. iv) 'Christopher Robin' plate, 235 mm diam., transfer printed and painted underglaze, No.14 of a 24 piece set. v) 'CHO-KR' ashtray, 80 mm diam., impressed mark 'CHO-KR PATENT' and marked 'S24', 'Patent Extinguishing CHO-KR Ashtray' transfer-printed. vi) coffee mug, 80 mm high, painted underglaze, marked 'C10'.*

as the 'Christopher Robin' nursery set or 'Canterbury Tales' series).

A series of face tankards modelled by Percy Metcalfe of famous politicians (such as Stanley Baldwin) were produced in white without any surface decoration save for the name of the face transfer-printed in black round the base of the tankard.

Shapes were generally simple and unadventurous, but their simplicity was effectively reinforced by striking use of bold monochrome colours. On tablewares, in particular, the simple shapes and bold colours were given a feeling of lightness and delicacy through the use of a thin translucent high glaze 9which was also used throughout the product range).

Colours ranged from a bright yellow, turquoise green, cerise etc., to a soft speckly beige and powder blue (similar to Moorcroft's).

**References**

*1) Leatherhead Museum, Church Street, Leatherhead, Surrey, has a good representative collection.*

*Selection of modelled pieces (courtesy of Leatherhead Museum). 1 to r:- i) Eastern lady, 125 mm high, by Phoebe Stabler, 1930, marked 'M37'. ii) Madonna and child, 210 mm high, by Phoebe Stabler, marked 'M34'. (loaned by Mrs. Hardenburg). iii) Child with staff, 135 mm high, by Phoebe Stabler, marked 'M38'. iv) 'Corn Girl', 190 mm high, by Allen G. Wyon, 1927, marked 'M72' (loaned by S.E.D. Fortescue).*

| Type of Ware | Production | Quality | Availability |
|---|---|---|---|
| all wares (excl. figures) | Moderate | Good | Uncommon |
| Figures | Low | Good to Very Good | Scarce |

**Marks**

Transfer-printed Ashtead Potters 1923-1935
(within outline of a tree on a hill)
± name of artist
+ pattern number (painted); Letter followed by a number :-
e.g. **J2** (jug 145mmx152mm); **B8** (bowl 50mmx152mm); **M1** (Metcalfe lion); **X7** (ink-well) 56mmx101mm). The number denotes the size.

+ colour code (painted):-
e.g. **a** dark green; **b** yellow; **c** Royal blue; **d** Celadon; **f** Powder blue; **g** ivory; **m** orange; **o** applegreen; **p** rose; **r** black; **s** mauve; **t** buff

On later wares:-
± transfer printed: BBCM/ASHTD
MADE + ENG
IN LAND

+ date codes, within "MADE IN ENGLAND" above (currently showing a cross). Codes noted so far are: a cross, square, triangle, quarter moon, swastiks (believed to represent 1928), anchor and star.

# ASHWORTH (1905-1913)

## G. L. Ashworth & Brothers (1862-1968) Hanley, Staffs.

Typical Wares: earthenware, glaze effects

## Historical Background and Products

**About 1845, the rights to use the title "Masons Ironstone" were bought from the china works of Charles James Mason & Co. by Francis Morley & Co., following Masons' bankruptcy. When Morley & Co. also got into financial difficulties, the Rochdale woollen firm of George L. Ashworth & Brothers took them over in 1962 together with the right to manufacture Mason's "Patent Ironstone China".**

With the collapse of the wool and cotton trade, G L Ashworth & Bros. was bought by the Goddard family, but continued to keep the company name as G L Ashworth & Bros.

J V Goddard started to experiment with flambe glazes, and rom 1905 high-fired lustres were produced under the direction of the Austrian chemist Dr. Basch.

Dr. Basch was appointed to produce "interesting" glazes, and a range of wares was produced with a variety of special glaze effects, some of which were known as *Lustrosa* and *Esterella*.

The quality of these wares was very good, and shapes were kept simple in order to show off the spectacular glaze effects. Mostly vases were decorated, in classical shapes, ranging from small, squat vases to larger urns.

Colours were generally monochrome, but with a striking colour palette, such as an apple green with a silky finish, for example, or a royal blue with white flecks and a high glaze. A deep maroon was a particularly impressive lustre glaze, similar in effect to Pilkington's *sunstone* glaze.

Dr. Basch's glazes were never marketed as planned, and Dr. Basch returned to Austria with the approach of the First World War.

In 1968, G L Ashworth traded as 'Masons Ironstone China Ltd.', and in 1973, Masons became part of Wedgwood, who currently maintain a collection of some 81 vases and 9 bowls.

**References**

*1)A collection at Masons Ironstone, Hanley, Staffordshire is open to view.*

| Types of Ware | Production | Quality | Availability |
|---|---|---|---|
| High fired lustres | Low | Very good to Excellent | Rare |

**Marks**

| | | |
|---|---|---|
| Impressed curve: | ASHWORTH | 1905-1913 |

± name of ware
e.g. LUSTROSA

± artists signature
printed underglaze
e.g. W Nash

*Vase, 260 mm high, marked 'Ashworth'.*

# WILLIAM AULT

## Swadlincote, Burton-on-Trent (1887 - 1975)

### Typical Wares: earthenware, pressed and moulded items

### Historical Background

**In 1887, William Ault left the Bretby Art Pottery and his partnership with Henry Tooth, and set up his own pottery at Swadlincote. He began to manufacture pottery similar to Linthorpe ware, which he termed *Ault faience*, though in the strictest sense of the word it was not actually faience. He experimented continuously with coloured glazes, and with the help of his daughters, Clarissa and Gertrude, applied them to pressed and moulded wares made at the pottery.**

In 1893, Ault won a gold medal at the Chicago 'World's Exposition' where he exhibited his already renowned plant pots. Ault's pieces lacked inventiveness however, and Christopher Dresser was commissioned to design pieces for the Ault pottery which were similar to the pieces that he designed for Linthorpe.

Towards the beginning of the First World War, coloured glazes were applied less frequently, as demand was for hand painted and highly decorated pottery. The Ault coloured glazes were revived somewhat in the 1920's and 30's, however, when the Ault Pottery produced some very fine art pieces.

In 1923, the firm was known as 'Ault and Tunnicliff', but later traded as 'Ault Potteries Ltd' until 1975.

### Products

A popular piece produced at the Ault Pottery was a vase supported by a metal stand (a design which was used as a trademark), but besides this and vases of many shapes and sizes, plant-pots and large jardinerès were the speciality of the pottery, and were produced in quantity from 1890. The pieces produced were of good quality and were offered for sale in the biscuit state, there being a choice of decoration.

Decoration was mostly in the form of coloured glazes (usually monochrome or bichrome), which tended to run into each other on the surfaces, but some sgraffito work was also executed.

About 1910, leadless glazes were introduced by Ault, which were supposed to be healthier for the decorators to work with. Some items of this time are marked *Ault's lead-less glaze*. After 1900, however, certain named wares were produced, such as *Sgraffito Ware*, *Creke Pattern* (a scroll motif on a red ground), *Mauresque Ware* (splashed and striated surfaces), *Ebonite Pattern* (an ebony-like black surface with stars and figures of clowns), *Anemone*, *Honesty*, *Iris*, *Bulrush*, etc.

The finer Ault pieces are difficult to come by, particularly those by Christopher Dresser. Dresser's designs include vases in South American styles, often streaked with a monochrome glaze. Dresser made good use of other media in his designs, such as metal handles and rims. His shapes vary from rounded forms (such as double-gourd vases) to a combination of rounded and angular forms (eg teapots).

The non avant-garde designs, such as those adopted for the jardineres, tended to be classically inspired. Although production was rather high of the garden wares, they are fairly scarce on the market. It could be that many of the unmarked pieces around are in fact Ault, but the same suggestion could equally apply to Bretby or Linthorpe items. One would have to make a very close scrutiny of styles to positively identify an unmarked piece.

**References**


1) *'A Tale of Three Potteries', by Roger Pinkham; The Antique Collector magazine; Sept., 1977.*

2) *Christopher Dresser. See under Linthorpe for references.*

*Pair of vases, hand-painted decoration, 165 mm high, impressed mark 'AULT ENGLAND', '9'.*

| **Type of Ware** | **Production** | **Quality** | **Availability** |
|---|---|---|---|
| Art wares signed by or attributed to Chr. Dresser | Low | Good to Excellent | Scarce |
| Other art wares (marked) | Moderate to High | Good | Uncommon to Scarce |

**Marks**
(NB: Not all Ault Pottery is marked)

| | | |
|---|---|---|
| Impressed or moulded: | AULT (a figure of vase) | 1887-1923 |
| | AULT | 1887-1923 |
| | R | 1887-1923 |
| ± 'AULT'S LEADLESS GLAZE' | (c.1910) | |
| ± 'Chr. Dresser' | (in impressed signature, sometimes moulded) See Linthorpe | |
| ± pattern number | (three numbers and a letter. It also occurs without a factory mark) | |
| ± 'ENGLAND' | (after 1891) | |

# BARON POTTERY

## Rolle Quay, near Barnstaple, Devon (1893-1939)

Typical Wares: earthenwares

### Historical Background

**William Leonard Baron formed his pottery at Rolle Quay near Barnstaple late in 1893, having previously worked for C H Brannam Ltd. since 1886. His ware was very similar to Brannam's *Barum Ware*, consisting of mostly vases, jugs and bowls with monochrome decoration.**

Considerable rivalry reigned between Baron and Brannam, particularly concerning Baron's enterprise in attracting coach loads of tourists to his pottery by erecting a sign outside the town and paying coach drivers a shilling for each load of passengers driven to his pottery.

The feud continued for some years, the similarity of the wares not helping matters. Baron continued to operate his pottery independently, however, until his death in 1938, when C H Brannam Ltd. absorbed the business, closing the works at Rolle Quay at the outbreak of war.

Some of Baron's better quality wares were exhibited at the British Industrial Arts Exhibition in 1920.

### Products

Baron Ware was produced in a variety of shapes and sizes, but a large proportion of the output consisted of pieces small in stature. This was because much of the ware was made for the Devon tourist market, and so many pieces bear written mottoes.

Apart from many pieces of simple shape, some vases were produced with twisted handles, similar in style to Brannam's. All the wares exhibit a high lead glaze over a red Devonshire clay body, giving a slight iridescence to pieces; but the quality of potting and decoration was somewhat lower than that of Brannam's.

Decoration was mostly in monochrome blues, greens or orange, but the finer art wares exhibit more intricate decoration, with relief modelled bird and floral designs.

*Vase, 315 mm high, marked '353'.*

**References**

*"The Artist Potters of Barnstaple" by Audrey Edgeler, to be published by Nimrod Publications, 1989.*

| Type of Ware | Production | Quality | Availability |
|---|---|---|---|
| Earthenware | Moderate to High | Poor to Good | Abundant |

**Marks**

| | | |
|---|---|---|
| Incised: | Baron, Barnstaple | 1899 - 1939 |
| ± Incised number, eg "70½" | | |

# C H BRANNAM

## Barnstaple, Devon (1855-1937)

### Typical Wares: earthenware (from 1879), terra-cotta

#### Historical Background

**In 1879, Charles Hubert Brannam, dissatisfied with the quality and type of ware manufactured at his father's pottery, took over the rental of the premises at Litchdon Street, Barnstaple, for the production of his own art pottery wares. He was 24 years old at the time, and had acquired his pottery education both in his father's workshops and at the Barnstaple School of Art. At the School he became acquainted with Alexander Lauder (1837-1921), who later set up his own pottery business nearby. Brannam realised the potential of the local red clay deposits at Fremington, and being a skilled potter already, set about producing a quality ware which would be acceptable to the discerning Victorian public. He initially produced jugs, toilet sets, vases and drain-pipes, to which he gave the name 'Barum Ware', after the Roman name for Barnstaple. Charles Brannam did most of the throwing himself, especially the art pieces, but had assistants to undertake the decoration.**

At first, primitive machinery was used, the ware being fired in a brick-built kiln, fed with faggots. A horse was employed for pulling the roller which prepared the clay.

In 1880, a contract was negotiated by Mr James of 'Howell & James', London, to market Barum Ware to London dealers. This heralded the success of Brannam's art ware, which soon won many local prizes, and gave the firm its Royal patronage in 1885. The ware then became known as *Royal Barum Ware.*

In 1882, Brannam took on a talented decorator by the name of James Dewdney, who produced some exceptional art vases. It soon became necessary however, to take on a second designer, and in 1886, William Leonard Baron was employed. Baron left in 1893, to set up his own pottery business in the vicinity, but not before contributing much to the success of the Brannam undertaking.

Barum Ware became extremely popular and was widely advertised. Pieces were sold at Liberty of London, and shown at international exhibitions. The price of a large jardinere in 1881 was thirty shillings, and a tall jar eighteen shillings, whilst smaller items could be purchased for seven or eight shillings.

Queen Victoria again patronised the pottery in 1892, as did many members of the Royal Family and European royal families on other occasions. In 1914, the pottery became a limited company, and wares from then on were stamped 'C H Brannam Ltd'.

*Two vases, marked 'LAUDER BARUM'. l to r:- i) 263 mm high; ii) 328 mm high.*

At the 1920 British Industrial Art Exhibition, Charles Brannam exhibited some fine examples of his work, particularly interesting of which was a range of toilet wares - some etched with bird and floral decorations, others decorated with scrolls, and covered with rich coloured glazes. Brannam were particularly successful in overcoming the difficulties of adapting the Devonshire red-body ware to such utilitarian purposes.

From 1920, the Fremington clay was purified by filter-pressing, and during the 1930's, production included moulded, pressed and cast items. Also during the 1930's, the firm earned the title 'By Royal Appointment to Her Majesty Queen Mary'. By then, the price of a large jardinere was fifty-two shillings and sixpence, whilst a tall 31-inch decorated vase (787 mm) was sixty-six shillings.

Charles Brannam died in 1937, aged 82. The pottery continues today, making mostly terra-cotta wares.

#### Products

Initially, the pots were decorated with a thin layer of white slip. The red clay body was exposed by sgraffito work, and then the glaze was applied. At first, the glaze employed was of a simple honey-coloured type, but later on, richer coloured lead glazes were developed.

The general style towards the turn of the century consisted of simple shapes decorated with coloured slips, with much carved and sgrafitto work depicting bird, fish and foliate subjects.

Much domestic pottery was manufactured, such as milk pans, and bread pancheons, whilst a large amount of flower pots were produced well into the 1930's. James Dewdney continued to decorate wares into the 1930's, assisted by Arthur Bradden. The decorations often consisted of flowers or foliage in low relief. Slip designs of birds, seaweed and animals were also popular, as was sgraffito work.

A great variety of items was made. A

catalogue of the 1930's shows decorated pedestals, pots and large vases "suitable for drawing rooms, halls and billiard rooms". Many have characteristic twisted handles applied to a simple shape, often decorated with stylised fish designs. The fish was a popular decorative subject, and sometimes appears as a moulded item, forming the spout of a jar or jug.

After 1918, the wares had become less decorated. The decoration on some items consisted only of a monochrome colour such as orange with a matt glazing, and had small twisted handles. Indeed, by the 1930's, much of the Barum Ware relied on its simplicity of shape and colour. The catalogue of this period names several colours, one of them being *Liberty Green*.

The 1930's saw an increase in the domestic product range, together with a decline in art wares. Wall plaques, salt cellars, candlesticks, ash trays, bulb bowls, grotesques, devil jugs, loving cups, toby jugs, fishmouth jugs, birdjugs, umbrella stands, ink pots, butter dishes, pen trays, sweet dishes - all were produced to order with a choice from 40 colourings. The collector will also come across terra-cotta garden wares dating from the 1930's.

Some light industrial wares were also manufactured, amongst which were heavy cloam ovens. The ovens were produced until 1939, and are still in evidence in some West Country houses today.

## Collecting Brannam Pottery

Brannam pieces are popular with collectors, not only for the interesting articles produced but also for their quality. Some of the pieces require much guesswork as to their purpose, and there is an impressive variety of small items available for collection.

Brannam ware is fairly plentiful on the antiques market, in keeping with the high output. Signed pieces are particularly sought after, and the earlier items with incised marks (1879 to 1898) are less common.

James Dewdney is certainly the most well known of the Brannam decorators, and his work exhibits an accomplished artistry. Signed pieces by him are not rare, as he was fairly prolific in his work, and the quality of his ware varies significantly.

Collectors should be wary of the similarity between Brannam ware and products of the neighbouring Lauder and Baron Potteries. The mark is often the only discernable difference. Certain minor Devon Potteries also produced wares similar to Brannam ware, and collectors may come across pieces from Edwin Beer Fishley's pottery at Fremington, for example.


**References**

1) *A Family Business - The Story of a Pottery, by Peter Brannam; pub. privately, 1982.*

2) *'The Artist Potters of Barnstaple' by Audrey Edgeler, to be pub. Nimrod Publications, 1989.*

3) *'Barum Ware - The Work of C H Brannam (1855-1937)' by Susan James; The Antique Collector magazine; Aug. 1973.*


| Type of ware | Production | Quality | Availability |
|---|---|---|---|
| Domestic items, often in single colours | High to Very High | Poor to Good | Common |
| Fine art wares, signed by C H Brannam or J Dewdney (1879-1898) | Moderate to High | Good to Very Good | Less Common |

**Marks**

| | | |
|---|---|---|
| Incised:<br>± date<br>± initials of decorator | C.H. Brannam<br>Barum | 1879-1898 |
| Impressed:<br>± '44561' (Reg. No.)<br>± 'MADE FOR LIBERTY & CO" (impressed) | C.H. BRANNAM<br>BARUM<br>N. DEVON | 1898-1930's |
| Printed or painted: | C. H. BRANNAM<br>LTD.<br>BARNSTAPLE | 1914-1955 |

(NB: Alexander Lauder imitated many of Brannam's styles from 1876 to 1916 at his Pottery at Pottington. His ware is marked 'Lauder Barum' ± date (c. 1880 - 1914)

**Artist's Marks** - incised

| | | |
|---|---|---|
| JD or J.D.<br>or | James Dewdney | 1882 - 1930's |
| W B | William Baron | 1886 - 1893 |
| F B | Frederick Baron<br>(son of William Baron) | 1897 - 1910 (approx) |
| A B | Arthur Bradden | |
| T L | Thomas Liverton | 1920's & 1930's |

# BRETBY ART POTTERY

## Woodville, Burton-on Trent (1883 to present)

Typical Wares: earthenware, pressed and moulded items

### Historical Background

**About 1882, Henry Tooth left the Linthorpe Art Pottery and went into partnership with William Ault, forming the Bretby Art Pottery in 1883. Wares produced were similar to those of Linthorpe, and being of reasonable price were popular. The quality was somewhat lower, though a few choice art pieces were made, and Bretby Ware was exhibited widely, and distributed to all the main retail outlets in Britain.**

William Ault did not stay long at Bretby. In 1886, he left the partnership to set up his own pottery nearby. Henry Tooth remained, however, and was assisted at the pottery by his son and daughters, one of which, Florence Tooth, proved to be a competent artist, who eventually ran the modelling shop.

About 1914, Henry Tooth's son took over the running of the pottery from his father. From this time and during the late 1920's the firm advertised as 'Tooth & Co.', and had a London showroom at Gamages in Holborn, the London pottery centre. In 1933, the pottery came into the possession of the Parker family, and continues today as 'Tooth & Company Ltd. Bretby Art Pottery', making and extensive range of wares from ornamental to horticultural.

### Products

A wide range of items was produced at Bretby, from very fine art pieces to general stock wares. Some of the stock wares were slip-cast or pressed and moulded. Plant pots, teapots and tobacco-jars were produced in quantity, whilst some vases were produced moulded in two halves.

The stock wares often had titles, such as *Ligna Ware* (moulded items resembling tree trunks), *Copperette Ware* (items resembling hammered copper pots), *Clanta Ware* (vases and bowls with black surfaces designed to resemble metal), *Jewelled Ware* (art deco itmes resembling metal with inlaid 'precious stones'), *Pastal Ware* (items with smooth surfaces and pastel colours), *Carved Bamboo Ware* (imitative of Japanese styles with relief modelled lines), *Ivorine* (similar styles to Carved Bamboo Ware), a form of cloisonne ware and *Nerton Ware*.

There were other wares which were not named, but were equally imitative of metals or ethnic styles.

The stock wares proved immensely popular, especially the Nerton Ware. Nerton Ware was produced in 1920 in five different colourings - green, rose, Royal blue, green and yellow. It was mottled, and is recognised by its streaky and chunky surfaces. The full range of Bretby art wares was made available for decoration in Nerton Ware, from small urns, pitchers and vases to umbrella stands and large jardineres.

Both colour and shape were simple on the many plant-pots produced, and 'dimpling' was a frequently used form of decoration on these items. Dimpling was the practice of depressing the sides of a bowl or vase at intervals. It was widely used at Burmantofts, Ault and Linthorpe, and may have been a remedy for 'correcting' badly thrown pieces.

As at Linthorpe, some of the glazes were multicoloured, but tended to be rather thick, such that the underlying details became obscured. Apparently, the glazes used were not of a type that would craze or crack. Certainly, the test of time has generally proved this to be the case.

About 1910, when the trend for oriental styles was evident, Bretby produced some interesting brown-based vases and jardineres, with a decoration in gold and pink lustre on matt black panels.

During the early 1930's, a successful range of ornamental wares was produced, such as *Peasant Pottery*, with incised patterns and a matt glaze. Another well

*Selection of wares. l to r:- i) lustre vase; ii) small jardinere; iii) small jardinere; tall vase, 325 mm high.*

thought of pattern was *Aquarius*, which comprised a fish motif, outline modelled with a plain glaze.

## Collecting Bretby Pottery

Bretby wares are plentiful on the antiques market at the time of writing, and prices are relatively low. A general style is evident that gives the wares an individuality of their own. The colours tend to be gaudy, even on the most artistic of pieces, and colour combinations are often oddly matched - cerise and yellow for example!

The current popularity of the house-plant and the functionality of Victorian jardineres have created a ready market for many Bretby pieces. Certainly, the quality of Bretby jardineres and planters in general, enables them to stand out from amongst the many hundreds of unmarked wares that were produced during the late-Victorian period.

**References**

1) *'A Tale of Three Potteries' by Roger Pinkham; article in the Antique Collector, September, 1977.*

2) *Tooth & Co. Ltd. Bretby Art Pottery, Woodville, Burton-on- Trent, Derbyshire.*

| Type of Ware | Production | Quality | Availability |
|---|---|---|---|
| Hand-thrown art pieces | Moderate to High | Good to Very Good | Common |
| Moulded and pressed items | High to very High | Poor to Very Good | Abundant |

The named wares are less common and generally of better quality. Bretby manufactured wares in a very wide quality range, making it difficult to give general assessments of quality.

**Marks**

Not all Bretby ware is marked, even modern pieces

Impressed:

1884-1890

(In conjunction with mark above) ENGLAND 1891 onwards

1883-1900 (Henry Tooth)

± title of ware, eg 'CLANTA', or 'CLANTA WARE'. c.1914

± pattern number

± artist's mark, eg Richard Joyce (later at Pilkington), Florence Tooth, William

Named Wares: 'Dickensian Ware' (1915-1920); 'Nerton Ware (1920); 'Jewelled Ware' (1900-1915); 'Copperette Ware' (1900-1915); 'Ligna Ware' and 'CLOISONNÉ WARE' (late 1890's); 'Carved Bamboo Ware' (from mid to late 1890's to early 1920's).

(ref. more detailed information on pattern numbers in Malcolm Haslam's excellent book 'English Art Pottery 1865-1915'.)

# BURMANTOFTS POTTERY

## Leeds (1880-1904)

### Typical Wares:
### thrown earthenware (faience), architectural faience, terra-cotta, moulded wares

### Historical Background

**The Burmantofts Works were established by Messrs. Wilcock & Co. in 1858 for the production of drain-pipes and fire-bricks, using a locally available grey-white clay.**

From 1879, the firm was managed by James Holroyd, who had previously been a woollen manufacturer. He commissioned the architect Maurice Bingham Adams in 1880 to design architectural faience, which heralded the start of the company's involvement in art pottery.

Work was exhibited at Howell & James showroom in London in 1881, and in 1882 the company produced their first catalogue entitled "A Catalogue of Architectural Faience and Decorative Terra-Cotta". By this time a large range of wares was being produced, from tiles, panels and fireplaces to vases and jardineres.

The early success of the firm is demonstrated by the expansion of the premises from four acres to fifteen in 1885. Commissions for Burmantofts architectural faience poured in, particularly for public buildings, notably the Metropole Hotel at Brighton (1889) and the National Liberal Club, Whitehall (1884).

By 1888, the firm had its own showrooms in Charterhouse Street, London. During the same year the firm was renamed 'The Burmantofts Company'. The name Burmantofts had been associated with the pottery for some time, and referred to the district in Leeds where the Works were situated. By 1889, however, the firm amalgamated with other Yorkshire enterprises, and became known as 'Leeds Fireclay Company Ltd.'. The same year, staff were taken on from the Linthorpe Pottery which had closed down.

In 1890, James Holroyd died, and was succeeded by one of his sons, also called James. Under the new management pieces were more widely exhibited and new retail outlets established (Liberty and Harrods, particularly).

With the turn of the century, public taste for art wares was dwindling, and in 1904, production of art pottery ceased at Burmantofts. The production of architectural faience continued until 1957, however, when the Works closed and the buildings were demolished.

### Products

For many years, architectural faience, glazed bricks and tiles were the main source of income for the pottery. The venture into art pottery (from 1880) produced pieces which closely followed the Linthorpe Pottery in characteristics, the early vases being plainly decorated with a single coloured glaze, and tending to be bulbous in shape with long necks. The glazes were translucent, and the colours bright.

The firm soon began to introduce surface designs, however, such as sgrafitto work and moulded decoration in relief. Most items were moulded, and included bowls and large jardineres as well as vases of every size. Pieces were fired at very high temperatures, producing hard, thickish glazes, and warm colours.

Some decoration was applique work in the form of hand-modelled animals and flowers. Some early crude wares exhibit a heavy applique form of decoration, similar to the French *barbotine* technique. The appearance of vases with twisting snakes and lizards amongst dense foliage is reminiscent of Palissy ware.

*Vase, 305 mm high, by V. Kremer, Persian style, marked 'Design 22', 'BURMANTOFT'S FAIENCE' and monogram for V.Kremer.*

Floral motifs were popular in Burmantofts decoration, and the chrysanthemum featured on many pieces made in the 1890's, as well as in copies of William De Morgan's *Persian* designs (many executed by V Kremer). Tiles were also produced at Burmantofts, not only in earthenware but also in terra-cotta. Tiles and terra-cotta panels were often decorated with the popular bird and floral motifs, and the *barbotine* style was also sometimes employed for panels.

Continental artists were among those employed at Burmantofts, notably V Kremer and B Sicard, who contributed to a distinctive style to many of the wares.

A series of African-style bottles and jars was produced, characterised by bold patterns and colours: gourd-shaped bottles (V. Kremer) and pilgrim bottles, in particular. Moorish patterns were also evident, appearing in Burmantofts catalogue until about 1900.

Other pieces made included flower-stands, water-bottles, lamp-bases, umbrella-stands, candlesticks, as well as the architectural products, such as fireplaces. As at the Ault Pottery, the coloured glazes tended to run on the surfaces. Large itmes, such as jardineres and umbrella-stands, particularly exhibit this feature. Production of jardineres was increased during the 1890's for what was a very buoyant market.

Non-moulded items are popular with collectors. The colours are extremely attractive, even in their usual monchrome, and range from brilliant turquoise blues to warm-toned russet-browns. Like Elton's colours, they are somewhat unique. Other glazes produced were a sang-de-boeuf (often made richer by being applied over a yellow slip), as well as some copper or silver lustres on dark red or blue grounds.

Some of the early bulbous vases were dimpled in shape (compare Bretby Pottery), but generally shapes were kept simple. The candlesticks and many of the jardinere pedestals were of an architectural style, with square bases and columnar features, and quite different from the rounded forms of other pieces. Many pieces are very large in size, reflecting the initial desire of Burmantofts to create large original wares.

After 1904, some modelled wares were produced by the Leeds Fireclay Company. These include animal figures, decorated in monchrome glazes, and are marked 'Lefico' (for Leeds Fireclay Co.).

Burmantofts pottery is attractive and was well produced, and good quality pieces command high prices today, particularly the early *barbotine* style *grotesques* or the later lustres.

**References**

1) *'Burmantofts Pottery'; catalogue of an exhibition at Cartwright Hall, Bradford; pub. Bradford Art Galleries & Museums, Nov. 1983.*

2) *Leeds City Museums and Abbey House Museum, Leeds.*

| Type of Ware | Production | Quality | Availability |
|---|---|---|---|
| Thrown faience | Moderate | Good to Very Good | Common |
| Tiles | High | Good | Uncommon |
| Moulded items (also termed 'faience') | High | Fair to Good | Common ('barbotine' style and decorated lustres: scarce) |

**Marks**

Impressed: BURMANTOFTS FAIENCE (*) 1880-1904

[mark] [mark] 1882 -1904

±'ENGLAND' (from the early 1890's)
± Pattern number
±artist's mark; e.g.

[mark] (V. Kremer)

(* lower case mark is early 1880's)

# BUSHEY HEATH POTTERY

## Bushey Heath, Herts.

Typical Wares: lustres (1923-33) similar to W De Morgan.

### Historical Background

**During the early 1900's, Henry Perrin acquired a large property at Bushey Heath, known as The Cottage. His wife, Ida Perrin, was an accomplished painter and water-colourist, and had trained in South Kensington and exhibited at the Royal Academy in London. She was a member of the Artists' Guild and Guild of Potters, and established a pottery at The Cottage, which became known as Bushey Heath Pottery. The pottery is noteworthy since a former partner of William De Morgan's, Fred Passenger, came to work from 1923 until the pottery closed in 1933.**

Encouraged by Mrs Perrin, Fred Passenger produced lustre pieces remarkably similar to De Morgan's lustre ware. In fact, Fred Passenger's pieces include the mark 'De M' within the Bushey Heath monogram, signifying that De Morgan's process was being employed.

The Perrins were prominent in the art and music circles of the time, and Ida Perrin spent much time living at the second family home in West Kensington. Ida Perrin lived to the age of 96, but her home The Cottage no longer exists. The site is now occupied by the Clay Lane Pumping Station.

### Products

Mostly lustre vases and bowls were produced. The pottery body is a fine white earthenware, somewhat porcellanous in texture. The lustres are particularly effective and of good quality, but the crafting and symmetry of shape are not as fine as De Morgan's work proper. The decoration by Frederick Passenger is mostly Isnik (Persian) inspired, with floriate and foliage motifs, also animals and fish.

*References*
*1) Leighton House Museum, 12 Holland Park Road, West Kensington.*
*2) Bushey Heath Museum, Bushey, Herts.*
*3) See also references under William De Morgan.*

*Bowl, 100 mm diam., purple, blue and silver lustre on porcelain, decorated inside with fish, marked 'Bushey Heath DM'.*

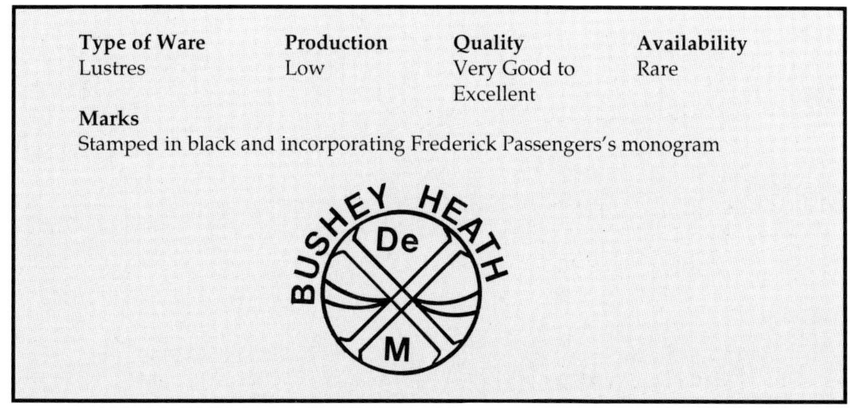

| Type of Ware | Production | Quality | Availability |
|---|---|---|---|
| Lustres | Low | Very Good to Excellent | Rare |

**Marks**
Stamped in black and incorporating Frederick Passengers's monogram

# CARLTON WARE (Wiltshaw & Robinson)

## Carlton Works, Stoke-on-Trent (1890 to present)

Typical Wares: art deco earthenware, porcelain, lustres

### Historical Background

**The Carlton Works were established about 1890 in Copeland Street, Stoke, by Wiltshaw & Robinson. Here,** *Carlton China* **was produced which was mostly of a domestic nature, but during the 1920's art pieces were produced in such varying styles that it is often difficult to identify a piece as belonging to a 'Carlton style'. All pieces were marked, however, and close examination should not cause any identification problem for the collector.**

The art pieces were well received, and the Company exhibited some fine examples at the British Industrial Arts Fair in 1920. Many of the art wares contained lustre decorations, and Wiltshaw & Robinson became renowned for their striking achievements with these glazes.

Novelty tablewares were produced from the mid 1920's, and many imitated leaves and vegetables in shape as well as decoration. Towards the end of the 1920's the Company had taken over the china firm of Birks Rawlins & Co., thus expanding their capabilities in the production of tablewares.

The Company was renamed 'Carlton Ware Limited' in 1958.

### Products

The great age of Carlton Ware was during the 1920's when many quality earthenware jugs and vases were produced alongside delicate tea and coffee services. A great deal of coloured porcelain was produced, often decorated against a black ground; and many interesting glazes were achieved, particularly lustres. Many of the designs were of Chinese influence, and were richly coloured. A *Cloisonne Ware* was produced in yellow and black, with a gold crazed background, and decorated with a Chinese pagoda pattern. Yellow and black seems to have been a favourite colour combination for the earthenwares, for floating- flower bowls were produced to match the Cloisonne Ware, and these were decorated with a black centre and yellow rim.

The discovery of Tutankhamen's tomb in 1922 prompted a range of Egyptian inspired pieces, and during the 1920's generally, a great variety of types and shapes were produced, from lamp bases to fruit bowls, wall plaques and ginger-jars. Many pieces were moulded, and lavish use of gulding was made as a complement to the decorations.

In 1920, a series of rouge flambe decorated pieces was launched, some of which were also decorated with a gold dragon. Another ware of the 1920's was *Armand*, which was a range of pale blue lustre ware.

Some of the art porcelain wares were brightly decorated, and coffee sets were produced with bright orange lustre interiors accompanying exterior designs of delicate pastel motifs. Some of the lustres were deep in colour, as exemplified by the range entitled *Rouge Royale*, and these were also often accompanied by lavish gilding or enamelling.

After 1925, some heavier earthenwares were produced, such as semi-grotesque jugs with relief moulded decoration; but there does not seem to have been any specialisation of product line. Some pieces had a high gloss glaze, whilst others bore a silky smooth glaze; some pieces were heavy and chunky in appearance, whilst others were light and delicate.

During the late 1920's, blue and mauve

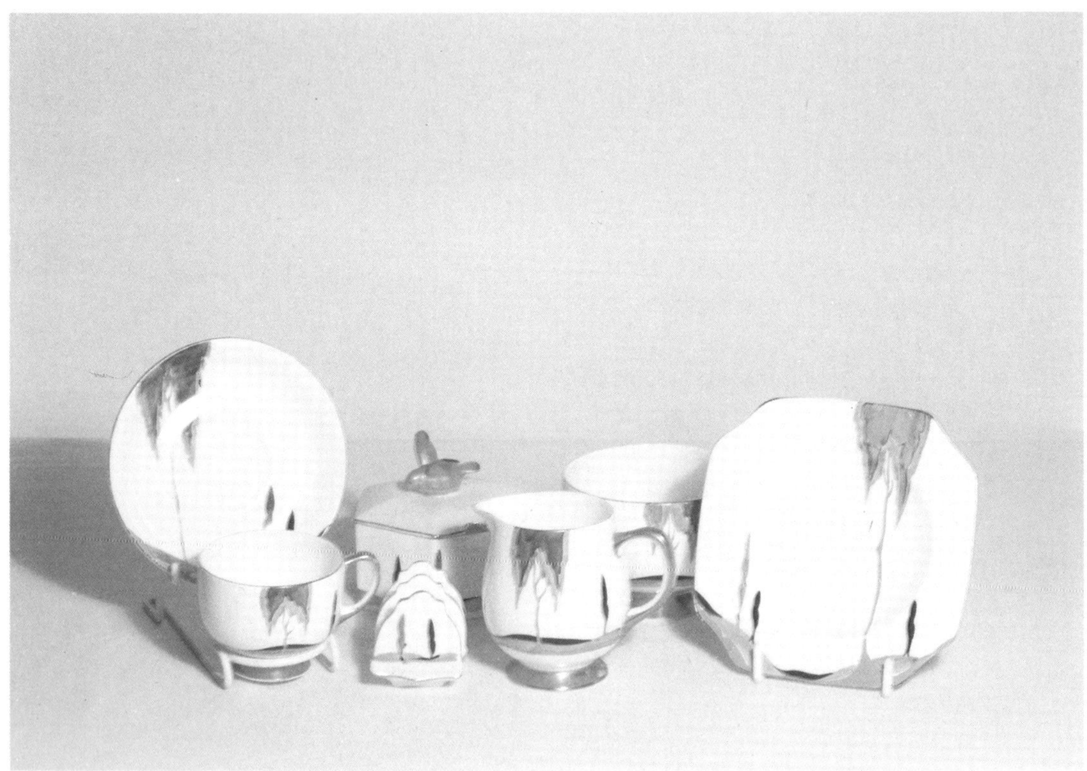

*Coffeeset in bone china*

were popular colours on Carlton pieces, and various types of bird often appeared as a decorative subject, such as a bluebird or kingfisher.

A popular range of art deco leaf shaped dishes and plates was produced in quantity. These often bore applique fruits in gaudy colours set against yellow or green embossed leaf backgrounds, each having a high glaze. Foxgloves and roses were also favourite decorations which appeared in relief on the various leaf shaped pieces. Most were sold in attractive individual cardboard boxes.

Much domestic ware was produced, and a large proportion was of good quality. The coffee sets produced in the 1920's, for example, with their bright lustrous interiors were as equal in quality to many of the tablewares produced by the more well known manufacturers during the same period.

**References**

*1) 'Carlton Ware: Naturalistic Patterns of the 1930's and 1940's; article by E Stirling in the journal of the Antique Collectors' Club, May, 1984.*

*Vase, 150 mm high, lustre and enamelled decoration.*

| Type of Ware | Production | Quality | Availability |
|---|---|---|---|
| Earthenwares | High | Fair to Very Good | Abundant |
| Porcelains | Moderate to High | Good to Very Good | Abundant |

NB: The quality range is large, such that the top quality pieces are attractive and sought after, but not so easy to come by as the lower quality pieces, of which there are many. Unfortunately, there is no information at present as to artists or designers at Carlton during the 1920-30 period.

**Marks**

Printed:

| | | |
|---|---|---|
| (Usually in black) | W & R<br>Stoke on Trent<br>CARLTON CHINA | 1906 onwards<br><br>(in circle + bird + crown) |
| (also **painted**) | Carlton Ware<br>MADE IN ENGLAND<br>Trade Mark' | 1925 onwards |
| | Carlton China<br>MADE IN ENGLAND | 1925 - 57 |

# CLARICE CLIFF, artist (b. 1899; d. 1972; fl. 1924-1939)

## A J Wilkinson Ltd
## Newport Pottery, Burslem.

Typical Wares: painted earthenware

### Historical Background

**Clarice Cliff trained as an artist at Burslem School of Art, and joined A J Wilkinson Ltd as an apprentice lithographer in 1916. Wages were low (about 5/7d per week including bus fares), and an amount was deducted for training for apprentices from the ages of 16 to 21.**

The special talents of Clarice Cliff were soon noticed by the owner of Wilkinson's, Colley Shorter, who arranged for her to study sculpture at the Royal College of Art, and then to experiment freely upon her return.

A J Wilkinson Ltd operated the Royal Staffordshire Pottery at Burlsem, and during the 1920's also acquired the adjoining Newport Pottery Company.

It was from this time that Clarice Cliff began to produce her famous art deco styles, mainly in the form of tea services. As sales for the then unusual pottery increased, production at Wilkingson's became concentrated on the Royal Staffordshire Pottery, whilst decoration was almost exclusively undertaken at the Newport Pottery, various areas being specially set aside for the new designs. The number of designs rose from 2 to 70, reaching a maximum of 150 by 1931.

About 1931, Clarice Cliff was made art director of both Wilkinson's Royal Staffordshire Pottery and their Newport Pottery subsidiary after successfully proving herself with her popular designs. During the 1920's, the company had a London Showroom at Holborn Viaduct, which at that time could be described as the mecca of pottery sales, and in 1934, Wilkinson exhibited pieces at Harrods' Exhibition of Modern Tableware.

Many wares were produced by Wilkinson in association with the Foley Pottery, and not all production was in the art deco style. Several fine flambe items were produced as well as pieces decorated in a chinese style. Wilkinson managed to cater for the popular market as well as the fine art market, and in the later 1930's produced many transfer-printed wares. With the outbreak of war in 1939, however, the selling of decorated pottery for the home market was banned, and with the removal of the labour force, the factory was closed.

### Products

Clarice Cliff started at the Newport Pottery Company by producing pieces of simple rounded shape, and decorating them with brightly coloured bands and diamond patterns. When these were found to sell well, she added circles, squares and primitive landscapes to her pattern range. Her colours were mostly reds, blues, greens, yellow and black, often on a yellow-ochre ground, and her landscapes were almost child-like in their simplicity. Shapes were often dramatic, but particularly appealing against the bold patterns of decoration.

Faults in the pieces created through poor potting were covered with lots of colour but generally, although the pottery body was poor, the decoration was good. Pieces were marketed under names such as *Bizarre, Ravel, Crocus, Scarab Blue, Inspiration Bizarre, Isis, Biarritz, Lodore, Fantasque* and *My Garden*.

*My Garden* pieces were characterised by brightly enamelled flower handles on vases, etc, whilst other designs incorporated stylised trees and flowers, sweetcorn, geometric motifs, sailing boats

*Tea-set, marked 'Bizarre', 'Honeyglaze Hand Painted'.*

and houses.

The *Crocus* pattern incorporated not only the flower, leaves and stalk, but also the roots and corm. It is a pattern much admired by collectors of this pottery.

Large jars and ginger-jars, painted with floral designs by Clarice Cliff in bright colours and gold (or abstract enamelled streaks), were produced under the title *Tibetan Ware*.

Many tea-sets were produced, having the characteristic yellow glazed surface, and during the 1930's angular shapes (especially conical) were evident. Some terra-cotta pieces were also produced and decorated in the same characteristic style. Some pieces were moulded, but the majority of Wilkinson's pottery was thrown.

During the early 1920's, Wilkinson manufactured a ware described as *Oriflamme*, with bright colours ranging from deep orange to pale blue.

Some art deco toilet sets decorated with black and white squares (pattern 6731) on a grey ground with art deco flowers attracted interest about this time, as did Wilkinson's imitations of Wedgwood's *butterfly lustres*. Interesting flambé vases and *saki* bowls were also produced by Wilkinson.

It is doubtful whether Clarice Cliff had anything personally to do with Wilkinson's productions other than those marked with her name and those produced during her period of art production.

Clarice Cliff also painted some fine dinner sets and other pieces from pottery designed by Frank Brangwyn (of Doulton), the artist Laura Knight, Paul Nash and M J Riach. These are generally of better quality than the more domestic Clarice Cliff ware.

## Collecting Clarice Cliff Pottery

Clarice Cliff wares are popular withcollectors of art deco, but prices tend to be high in relation to the quantity and quality of the ware. Many dealers tend to forget that the vast proportion of Clarice Cliff pottery consisted of sets - teasets, dinner sets, etc. 'One-off' studio pieces are scarce and are usually in the form of large vases, ginger-jars, etc. Individual pieces from sets are plentiful, however.

*Jug, 177 mm high, marked 'Bizarre'.*

**References**


*1) Clarice Cliff - The Bizarre Affair, By Louis K Meisel; pub. Thames & Hudson, 1988.*

*2) Collecting Clarice Cliff, by Howard Watson; pub. Kevin Francis, 1988.*

*3) Clarice Cliff, by Peter Wentworth; pub. L'Odeon, 1976 & 1981.*

*4) The Colourful World of Clarice Cliff, by Howard Watson; pub. Kevin Francis, 1989*

*5) 'Clarice Cliff'; catalogue of an Exhibition at the Museum & Art Gallery, Brighton, 1972.*

*6) 'Commercial Courage'; article by Pat Watson in the Antique Dealer & Collector, August, 1988.*


| **Type of Ware** | **Production** | **Quality** | **Availability** |
|---|---|---|---|
| Domestic Wares | High to Very High | Poor to Good | Abundant |
| Fine art pieces | High | Good to Very Good | Common |

**Marks**

| Transfer printed: | Clarice Cliff<br>WILKINSON LTD<br>ENGLAND | c.1930-1939 |
|---|---|---|

± design name, eg: 'Bizarre by Clarice Cliff'.
± designer's name

NB: The Clarice Cliff mark may incorporate the legend 'Newport Pottery & Co', or the name 'Royal Staffordshire' may appear on its own. Information is not yet available to precisely date the variations.

# CRAVEN DUNNILL & CO. LTD.

## Jackfield, Shropshire (1871-1951)

Typical Wares: tiles, art pottery, lustres

### Historical Background & Products

**Craven Dunnill & Company (formerly Hargreaves & Craven) was formed in 1871, and produced tiles using similar processes to Maw & Co., nearby. (ref. MAW & CO.)**

Craven Dunnill were well known for their copies of medieval lustred tiles for the home or church, a speciality which won them numerous commissions, not only for restorations but also for new buildings in the Gothic revival style so popular during the latter part of the 19th. century. The Roman Catholic Cathedral at Shrewsbury was one of their commissions, and is a good example of the Company's encaustic tile work.

The majority of tiles produced seem to have been mostly decorated with floral motifs. Greens, browns, pink and yellow-ochre were common colours utilised, often as monochrome decoration. The colour and style of decoration varied with the process of tile production. Some relief-moulded tiles often had a monochrome translucent glaze, such as green, whilst others would have been underglaze printed (again possibly in monochrome), on-glaze transfer-printed, or produced by a variety of processes.

Tile sizes were mostly six inch square. An eight inch square series of twelve tiles featured animal portraits, printed with a border, in blue. Few pictorial tiles, however, seem to have been produced, and those that were vary considerably in subject matter and style. A catalogue for 1879 shows several designs, from transfer-printed subjects in outline, such as buildings or scenes, to quite intricate Victorian conversation pieces elaborately moulded.

Very little is known about the operation of the Company, and much research still needs to be done. For a short period, Craven Dunnill ventured into art pottery, and some rare pieces are on display at Jackfield Tile Museum, along with several examples of the Company's tiles.

Art pottery so far discovered has been similar to Maw & Company's wares, with lustre decoration on blanks bought in, mainly from the Staffordhire Pottery of Thomas Forester & Sons, Fenton, Longton.

Not all Craven Dunnill's art pottery is marked, however, although many pieces bear the impressed mark of Thomas Forester & Sons.

The quality of decoration was good, but not quite as fine as that of Maw & Co., although similar designs were employed. Mostly vases were decorated.

**References**


*1) Jackfield Tile Museum, Ironbridge.*
*2) Clive House Museum, Shrewsbury (tiles and vases).*
*3) The Roman Catholic Cathedral, Shrewsbury (tiles).*

*Pair of vases, 188 mm, yellow lustre, marked with a transfer print in black underglaze CRAVEN DUNNILL & CO. JACKFIELD.*

| Type of Ware | Production | Quality | Availability |
|---|---|---|---|
| Tiles | Moderate to High | Good | Abundant |
| Art Pottery | Very Low | Good | Rare |

**Marks**

Impressed:
(Tiles)

Craven Dunnill & Co.
(plus a drawing of the factory)
JACKFIELD

± 'Salop'

Transfer printed in black:
(art pottery)

CRAVEN DUNNILL & CO. JACKFIELD

Painted:
(art pottery) C. D. + Co. J (with shield)

± 'FORESTER' impressed

# WILLIAM DE MORGAN (artist/potter)

## Typical Wares : art pottery (1869 - 1907), lustres, enamels

### Historical Background

**To many, William De Morgan was a symbol of the rennaissance of British pottery, releasing it from the many dull, monotonous styles that had pervaded for so long. Through relentless experimentation, he contributed much to ceramic art, leaving behind many fine pieces which set the standard of art pottery for the future.**

His pottery is therefore something of an historical landmark, not only for the various ceramic achievements that it exhibits but also for its style and decoration, which were closely linked to the development of the Arts and Crafts movement in this country. De Morgan was a founder member of the Arts and Crafts Exhibition Society, and was a close friend of other pioneers in the movement, notably William Morris, the textile designer and Edward Burne-Jones, the painter. Both these friends had some influence on De Morgain's pottery decoration.

De Morgan was educated as an artist at the Royal Academy Schools from 1859 to 1861, after leaving which he began to design stained glass. In 1869, he constructed a pottery kiln at the family home in Fitzroy Square, London, for the production of tiles to his own design. He began solely as a decorator of pottery, decorating pieces manufactured for him in Staffordshire (mostly by J H & J Davis), and tiles manufactured as white blanks from Holland.

Besides the decoration of tiles and other ceramics, he experimented in metallic pigments and lustre colours, reviving older processes, and imitating oriental and medieval designs. His lustre colours were based on copper and silver, and were produced by a complicated process of high temperature reduction in the kiln. He also developed a series of non-lustre colours from metallic oxides, which he termed *Persian Colours*.

In 1872 he moved production to Cheyne Row, Chelsea, incorporating a showroom for his ware. Vases, plates and bottles were produced, alongside the continued decoration of tiles. His pieces gradually became known and the business expanded, necessitating the employment of three assistants: Frank Iles as kiln operator, and Charles and Fred Passenger as decorators. Several commissions were undertaken, notably the completion of missing Islamic tiles at Lord Leighton's 'Arabian Hall' in Kensington, the decoration of the 'Tabard Inn' at Turnham Green, London, and designs for P & O Steamships.

From 1882 to 1888, De Morgan carried on the expanding business at Merton Abbey; but in 1888 he moved to Townmead Road, Sands End, Fulham, where he went into partnership with the architect Halsey Ricardo. Here De Morgan developed a process of *double-lustering* which gave increased depth to his pieces. He also succeeded in decorating wares with two tones of lustre.

De Morgan's partnership with Ricardo prompted an increase in the production of 'art tiles'. Ricardo advocated, with William Morris, that city buildings could be make to look brighter with exterior tile decoration. The partnership lasted 10 years, during which time De Morgan created his finest pieces. The high quality of output was achieved through the use of new equipment (designed by De Morgan himself) and through continued experiment with chemical processes.

From 1892, De Morgan began to winter in Florence for health reasons, but managed to send back designs to London by post. In 1898 he formed a new partnership with Frank Iles and the Passenger brothers, which continued until 1907, when the pottery closed. Frank Iles and the Passenger brothers then moved

*Tazza, 230 mm diam., blue lustre by Fred Passenger, marked solely 'FP'.*

away, but continued to decorate pottery until 1933 (see also 'Bushey Heath Pottery'). After De Morgan retired, aged 68 in 1907, he took up novel writing, and was highly successful. He died in 1917, having contracted trench- fever through conversing with a war witness about the fighting at the Front.

## Products

De Morgan's pottery is highly distinctive, exhibiting great artistry in its decoration. It is thus eagerly sought after by collectors, and commands extremely high prices. The Persian Colours are vivid, and the lustres (De Morgan's favourite means of decoration) are spectacular.

Whilst the earlier wares were decorated on a plain white background, later wares were on a deep blue background. The decoration itself tends to be bright, and covers the entire surface of a piece, favourite subjects being exotic flowers, medieval galleons, and animals.

The non-lustre glazes are high, but the lustre glazes are smooth to the touch and exhibit an iridescence rather than a deep reflection. They are therefore completely different from the Pilkington Pottery's lustres, which have a high reflective surface.

The Fulham period saw the production of the finest quality lustres. The copper oxides used produced a ruby lustre, whilst the silver oxides gave a yellow or bluish-silver lustre. The 'Persian Colours' were actually enamels painted on a white cracked slip, and ranged from turquoise to red, purple, yellow and green.

The deer was a favourite animal form of decoration on De Morgan's work. On plates, the animal was often depicted in non-lustre colours against a lustre background of oak leaves or indefinite foliage. When this was achieved in monochrome, the effect obtained negated the need for a two colour contrast, the non-lustre against lustre providing all the necessary depth. Rabbits, birds and fish were also regularly depicted, as were exotic and mythical creatures.

De Morgan's shapes appear to conform to a characteristic style, with rounded forms being predominant. Bowls are often deep with steeply rounded sides, and vases are sometimes gourd-like, occasionally with domed covers.

The early Staffordshire pieces (decorated during the Chelsea and Merton periods) comprise mostly chargers, with wide flat rims and scooped centres. Because of their resemblance to Cardinals' hats these chargers are often referred to as Cardinal hat plates. Decoration is usually continued on the reverse of these chargers, a characteristic typical of all De Morgan's art ware (and also of the Pilkington Pottery). These early pieces are more commonly found with an overall ruby lustre over a white slip. Yellow lustre was less commonly employed on these wares.

A F Wenger decorated some of De Morgan's designs in lustre colours at Hanley, around 1911. The pieces are mostly plates, incorporating De Morgan's stag designs or abstract geometrical patterns, and sometimes, but not always, marked with the initials 'AFW' in monogram, often accompanied by the name 'Furnivals, Burslem' stamped on the base. As these pieces tended to be proofs and try-outs of glazes, many also bear the name or number of the glaze. The Wenger family sold glaze materials to De Morgan, but it is not known how many of the proof pieces are in existence.

| Type of Ware | Production | Quality | Availability |
|---|---|---|---|
| Tiles | High | Moderate to Good | Uncommon |
| Other Wares (Mostly vases, plates and bowls) | Low | Very good to excellent | Rare, especially lustres |

**Marks**

1 Impressed: J H & J DAVIS ( may also include an impressed capital letter such as H or W)
Early decorated Staffordshire blanks (1869 to approximately 1882) unsigned by de Morgan.

2 Impressed: painted or printed:

W. DE MORGAN

DE MORGAN

WDE

DM

De M

D I P (De Morgan, Iles and Passenger)

W. DE MORGAN & CO

± name of pottery location:

1882 - 1888 - Merton Abbey
1888 - 1907 - Sand's End

(items marked 'Bushey Heath' were decorated by Fred Passenger 1923-33)

± painted artist's initials from 1879:

FP - Fred Passenger

CP - Charles Passenger

JJ - Joe Juster

JH - Jim Hersey

MJ - M Juster

HR - Halsey Ricardo

**References**


*1) Lord Leighton's Arabian Hall is open to the public at the Leighton House Museum, 12, Holland Park Road, West Kensington, London.*
*2) The Tabard Inn, Turnham Green, London. The public house is near the Underground Station in Bath Road. Tiles may be seen in the entrance porch and upstairs.*
*3) The Victoria & Albert Museum, London.*
*4) Tiles may still be seen in some of the porches of houses in Chiswick Mall, and at Sands End, near Putney Bridge. 'De Morgan Road' appropriately commemorates the potter.*
*5) Cardiff Castle has a collection of various pieces by William De Morgan.*
*6) The William Morris Gallery, Forest Road, Walthamstow, London E17, houses a collection of De Morgan pottery.* *7)'William De Morgan Tiles', by J Catleugh; pub. Trefoil, 1983.*
*8) 'William De Morgan', by W Gaunt & M D E Clayton-Smith; pub. Studio Vista, 1971.*
*9) 'William De Morgan (1839-1917)'; Catalogue of an exhibition at Leighton House, 1972; pub. De Morgan Foundation.*
*10) 'Catalogue of Pottery by William De Morgan', by Roger Pinkham; pub. Victoria & Albert Museum, London, 1973.*
*11) 'The Designs of William De Morgan', catalogue by Martin Greenwood, pub. Richard Dennis & William E. Wiltshire III, 1989, to coincide with an exhibition at the V&A.*

# DELLA ROBBIA POTTERY

## 2A, Price Street, Birkenhead (1894 - 1906)

Typical Wares: modelled and hollow wares, chargers, architectural wares (plaques, mosaics), tiles, ecclesiastical statuary

### Historical Background

**The Della Robbia Pottery was founded in 1894 by the sculptor Conrad Dressler and the artist Harold Rathbone (who was a former pupil of Ford Madox Brown). The pottery took its name from the 15th Century Italian family of Della Robbia, who produced *faience* during the period of the Italian Renaissance.**

The pottery was the main part of an enterprise which also included metal work and wood carving, and employed artists from local schools of art. About fifteen people were employed at one time in the pottery production, and included the artist Robert Anning Bell and the Italian sculptor Carlo Manzoni.

Harold Rathbone found affinity with many of the exponents of the Arts and Crafts movement, and, although the original purpose of the pottery was to produce solely architectural pieces, Rathbone's ideas were not readily accepted by architects at the time.

The work was exhibited widely, however, and found favour in high places; items were purchased by King George V when he was Duke of York, and also by Queen Victoria and Edward VII. Other famous purchasers included the musician Paderewski and the actress Sarah Bernhardt.

Rathbone was keen to promote many of the principles adopted by the Arts and Crafts movement, such as practical hand-made wares, as a reaction against the machine age. He also took a liberal approach to his workforce, allowing them a certain freedom of expression in their work. Outlets for the products were through Liberty and Morris & Co. in London, as well as outlets in New York, Paris and locally in Liverpool.

In 1897, Conrad Dressler left the pottery to found his own pottery at Great Marlow (The Medmenham Pottery). He was replaced by the sculptor Carlo Manzoni, who closed his own concern (the Granville Pottery) in order to join Della Robbia.

In 1900, the pottery amalgamated with the ecclesiastical and architectural firm of the sculptor Emile de Caluwe, hoping to exploit a profitable market in monumental gravestones, etc.

In spite of producing art pottery which was popular, the pottery itself was never commercially successful, and Della Robbia closed in 1906. The architectural side of the business was a failure in comparison to the production of other wares, but Rathbone's general lack of business sense seems to have been a prime cause of closure.

### Products

Wares produced were of good quality decoratively, though the pottery body was poor. It seems that there were often problems with the clays used, which were mostly red in colour and sometimes white, depending on the source.

The artists employed at Della Robbia proved to be both competent and faithful to the Italian Renaissance style. One designer, Miss Aphra Peirce, produced some noticeably original work, and the artist Annie Smith decorated some fine plates, one of which, dated 1895, bears the figure of a griffin. Liza Wilkins decorated many fine vases, often with figures or animal heads attached in relief, and Harold Rathbone himself threw and decorated many pieces, which are also of good quality. Cassandia Annie Walker was one of the more prolific artists at the pottery, and produced many high quality pieces, mostly in the art nouveau style.

Many vases, jugs, plates and chargers were produced, some featuring grotesques. Painting and sgraffito work were the main decorative form and some pieces were mounted with silver. The red pottery body was coated with a white slip, upon which the sgraffito work was undertaken, the colour being applied

*Two vases by Charles Collis. l to r:- i) vase and cover, 165 mm high. ii) vase, 280 mm high, dated 1900.*

afterwards. The painted colour were bright, mainly reds and greens, and glazes were usually clear.

Besides the Italian influence, there was a clear Middle Eastern flavour, and some designs depicted Islamic motifs. Medieval and Celtic designs were also present, as well as the more usual art nouveau and pre-Raphaelite inspired decorations.

Wares also included pottery panels modelled in high relief with figures. These were frequently given titles, such as *King Alfred*, and *Isaac*, and were sculptured by Harold Rathbone, Carlo Manzoni, Ellen Mary Rope, Robert Anning Bell and Conrad Dressler in particular. These architectural wares were part of a large range which included window-boxes, fountains, sun-dials and ecclesiastical statuary (from 1900).

## Collecting Della Robbia Pottery

The short life of the pottery has made pieces uncommon, so much so that many pieces command high prices today, particularly the architectural wares. The collectability of Della Robbia, however, is more a reflection of its individuality of design, the italianate styles with their vivid colours making a striking contrast to other wares of the same period.

Collectors should note, however, that the quality of work varies widely, reflecting the various talents of the artists and throwers employed.

**References**

*1) Birkenhead Central Library has some examples of pottery panels.*

*2) The work of Carlo Manzoni is shown in two sculpted figures above the entrance to the Midland Bank in Charing Cross, London.*

*3) The Memorial Church, Manor Road, Wallasey, has some panels by Conrad Dressler.*

*4) The Williamson Art Gallery, Birkenhead, has some pieces.*

*5) Della Robbia Pottery, Birkenhead 1894-1906, An Interim Report; produced by the Williamson Art Gallery & Museum; pub. Metropolitan Borough of Wirral, c.1974.*

*6) Catalogue of an Exhibition in 1980 entitled 'The Birkenhead Della Robbia Pottery, 1893 (sic) - 1906'; pub. Jeremy Cooper Ltd.*

*Plaque, 490 mm wide, marked 'LJ', '102', and dated 1906.*

| Type of Ware | Production | Quality | Availability |
|---|---|---|---|
| Hollow wares | Low to Moderate | Poor to Excellent (pottery body poor) | Uncommon |
| Architectural wares | Low to Moderate | Good to Excellent | Scarce |

**Marks**

| Incised and painted: | a medieval sailing ship varying in style (usually green) with the letters D R to the left and right (usually in red) | 1894-1906 |
|---|---|---|

± date (as year) under the factory mark
± throwers monogram (normally incised)
± pattern number (1 to at least 1050)
± artist's initials painted, of which the following is a selection:-

| | |
|---|---|
| AB | Annie Beaumont |
| AP | Aphra Peirce |
| AS | Annie Smith |
| C | Charles Collis |
| CAW (or CW) | Cassandia Annie Walker |
| EMR | Ellen Mary Rope |
| GR | Gertrude Russell |
| HR | Harold Rathbone |
| LW | Liza Wilkins |
| M de C | Marianne de Caluwé (wife of Emile de Caluwé) |
| RB | Ruth Bare |

N.B. Carlo Manzoni and Conrad Dressler do not appear to have marked their work.

# DOULTON & CO

## Lambeth & Burslem

Typical Wares: art wares 1860 to present, saltglaze stoneware, earthenware, faience, silica stoneware, rouge flambé.

### Historical Background

**Doulton began in 1815, when John Doulton and John Watts founded the firm of 'Doulton & Watts' at Lambeth in London for the production of brown salt-glaze stoneware. The items produced were mainly drinking vessels, plaques and chemical jars, but drainpipes were manufactured as a single concern by John Doulton's brother Henry. When John Watts retired in 1853, Henry Doulton's drainpipe business merged with Doulton & Watts to form 'Doulton & Company'.**

At the time, there were several saltglaze stoneware potteries in the Lambeth area all making similar wares; it was not until much later that the art pottery side of the business began. After exhibiting some experimental pieces of stoneware at the Paris Exhibition of 1867, and having had them well received, Henry Doulton engaged a student artist from the Lambeth School of Art by the name of George Tinworth. Tinworth's task was to undertake stoneware plaque modelling and terra-cotta work to his own design; and he soon became renowned in the art of stoneware modelling.

In 1871, another student from the Lambeth School of Art was employed, Hannah Barlow, who had previously spent a short time at the ill-fated Minton's Art Pottery Studio in Kensington. She was engaged as an artist, and was soon joined at Doulton by her brother Arthur Barlow.

As the company expanded, more student artists were engaged for studio work, notably, Hannah Barlow's sister, Florence (in 1873) and Frank Butler. Arthur Barlow died in 1878, but by 1881 there were 36 artist-decorators and modellers employed at Doulton which, together with many assistants, indicates the profitable state of the business at this time.

In 1878, Doulton & Co. purchased the Pinder Bourne & Co. works at Burslem in Staffordshire for the production of pottery blanks which would subsequently be decorated at Lambeth. From 1884, painted china was also produced at the Burslem factory.

The 1870-90 period saw Doulton at their best in terms of artistry. They had, after all, the cream of English decorators and modellers. In 1880, Mark V Marshall joined Doulton as a decorator. He had previously worked for the Martin Brothers, but whilst at Doulton he modelled many fine animal studies. Of the many women artists employed, Eliza Simmance became renowned for her art-nouveau style flower and fruit paintings, whilst during the 1870's, Emily J Edwards showed great artistry in her formal incised decoration of simple lines and foliage.

*Selection of Lambeth wares. l to r:- i) vase, 275 mm high, by George Tinworth (monogram on body). ii) vase, 210 mm high, 'Carrara Ware', by Edith Lupton. iii) vase, 287 mm high, by Frank Butler.*

Technical achievements were also being made at Doulton during this time, and during the 1880's, William Rix played an important part in evolving coloured glazes which would withstand the great heat of the saltglaze stoneware kilns. The range of decorative colours was therefore extended, and the scene was set for further experimentation culminating in some of the finest technical achievements in the history of pottery.

During the late 1890's and the early 1900's, Charles J Noke (previously of the Worcester Porcelain Company), together with Doulton's art director, John Slater, began to experiment with *rouge flambe* and *sang-de-boeuf* glazes on Chinese ceramics. The revival of these oriental glazes was technically difficult since a precise temperature control was required in the kiln. In 1901, however, Cuthbert Bailey, assisting the team, was able to control the reducing process to such an extent that *flambe* wares could be produced not only with certainty but also in quantity. The work took three years before any pieces could be produced for sale; and Bailey was assisted in his research by Bernard Moore, who was later to produce his own flambe wares. The new flambe was first exhibited at the St. Louis Exhibition in the United States in 1904, and was an immediate success. Each piece was more or less unique, the streaks and mottles apparently matching the quality of the finest antique Chinese specimens.

From 1907, the production of decorated saltglaze stoneware at Lambeth gradually diminished. It began to lose its appeal because of its heaviness in appearance and colour. Doulton therefore decided that a different range of products was called for, and so the 'Lambeth Art Wares' were promoted. Meanwhile, Noke was further experimenting in flambé by extending the colour range, sometimes coating the glaze with metallic oxides. He termed the latter *Sung Ware* after the Chinese dynasty of the same name. It was widely advertised in the early 1920's, and much favoured by George V and Queen Mary. *Sung Ware* was shown at the British Industrial Arts Exhibition of 1920, where Doulton's exhibit was described as 'a handsome exhibit charmingly displayed'.

During the 1920's Charles Noke was joined in his experiments by Cecil Noke (his son) and Harry Nixon. Through research into high- temperature fired glazes, they produced *Chang Ware* in 1925. This had a heavier body than *Sung Ware* and was brightly coloured with thick congealed glazes. Bailey and Noke also experimented with crystalline glazes, applying them to a high- temperature zinc-oxide ceramic body. Production was limited, as special kilns had to be used in order to maintain a steady temperature of 1400 C for several hours. A slow cooling was then induced to allow crystals to grow. Pieces are therefore rare, and consist principally of small vases, which have a whitish background, but little other decoration. Their production was discontinued in 1914, and they rank amongst the rarest items of Doulton pottery. Charles Noke eventually retired in 1936, having gained much acclaim for Doulton in the field of art wares.

During the late 1920's and 1930's, Frank Brangwyn was designing pottery for Doulton, of a style completely different to Noke's. Brangwyn was once an assistant to William Morris, and produced items for Doulton under the Royal Doulton *Brangwynware* mark. He was knighted in 1941.

In 1956, production of salt-glazed stoneware ceased, and the Lambeth Pottery moved production to Burslem, where art pottery is still made today, alongside the production of domestic ware.

## Products

The early salt-glazed stoneware was decorated in cobalt blue, but by the early 1870's greens and browns were also used. The designs were incised on to jugs and vases, and consisted chiefly of animals, birds and leaf scrolls, for which the Barlows were renowned. Artists and modellers often shared work on any one piece, such that the decorations might include a variety of ornamentation, from embossed, beaded or incised (sgraffito) work.

Distinguished modellers included George Tinworth, who studied at the Lambeth School of Art with Robert Wallace Martin (animal groups and stoneware figurines), and Leslie Harradine, who later modelled some of

| Type of Ware | Production | Quality | Availability |
|---|---|---|---|
| Saltglaze stoneware | Very High | Poor to Good | Fairly Abundant |
| Named wares, eg 'Holbein Ware' | Low to Moderate | Good to Excellent | Common |
| modelled wares | Low to Moderate | Good to Very Good | Common |
| faience | Moderate to High | Good to Very Good | Common |
| flambés, sang-de-boeuf | Low to Moderate | Good to Excellent | Uncommon |
| crystalline glaze | Very Low | Very Good | Very Rare |
| named flambés, eg 'Sung' | Low | Very Good to Excellent | Scarce |
| earthenware | Moderate to High | Good | Common |

**Marks**

Until 1882, each example of artistic stoneware produced at Doulton was original and unique. From 1882, some designs were produced in series by assistants. These are marked 'x' followed by a number.

All Doulton pieces are marked, especially by the artists who decorated them. Two albums of artists' marks from 1871 to 1881 were presented to Henry Doulton by the artists themselves.

Charles Noke's designs. Signed pieces (usually with initials in monogram) are much sought after, but as output tended to be rather high during this early period, individuality was not generally recognised.

Painting increased as a means of decoration at Doulton in the late 1880's and 1890's. The range of colours was increased, extending to yellows and pinks, and decoration included more surface texture work. Eliza Banks was renowned for her painting on stoneware using the pâte-sur-pâte method.

Besides the stoneware, Doulton produced many other types of ware, including varieties of faience. The fashion of the time demanded less sombre decoration, and the faience consisted of bright colours painted on to a smooth pottery surface. It was fired a minimum of three times; and the work was carried on separately at the Doulton Art Studios from 1874 by such artists as Minna Crawley, Mary Butterton, and Florence and Esther Lewis, who all painted the classical floral designs in vases and wall plaques. The Lewis's also painted landscapes and bird groups.

Between 1880 and 1912, Doulton & Co. were also producing a *Silicon* ware. It was a smooth, hard form of stoneware, which was liberally decorated by such artists as Eliza Simmance and Edith Lupton. Being a high quality production, *Silicon Ware* was successful, such that Doulton began to produce a whole series of quality wares towards the turn of the century. These included, *Carrara Ware* (1887-1896) - a white marble-like stone- ware; *Crown Lambeth Ware* (1892-1900) - a rare fine-textured earthenware with a real ivory tint; *Impasto Ware* (1879-1906) - a ware decorated by use of coloured 'slips'; *Chine Ware* (1886-1914) - a ware decorated by pressing lace into the soft clay; *Marqueterie Ware* (1886-1906) - a ware in which the body of the pot was built up with a mosaic of coloured clays, similar to marquetry work. This latter ware is particularly rare, since the process involved was technically difficult, necessitating many firings in the kiln.

The *Sung* and *Chang* wares are highly prized by collectors, and exhibit much variety of colour. The flambé wares reveal several characteristics, a typical example being *landscape flambé*, in which pastoral and other scenes are set in a dark tone, merging into a polished red background. Landscapes vary from high quality on large vases to poorer quality on smaller items such as ash-trays.

Many other types of ware were produced at Doulton during the latter part of the 19th century, including delicately proportioned miniature vases, and sporting and commemorative wares.

In 1906, Noke introduced a series based on Ingoldsby's poem 'The Jackdaw of Rheims'. This was somewhat of a success and was produced mainly on vases, jugs, trays and other small pieces. Other series followed, including *Dickens Ware* (scenes from Dickens' novels), *Shakespeare* (scenes from Shakespeare's plays), *Bayeux Tapestry*, *Old Coaching Scenes*, etc. Some were produced on jardinères, which gave a larger expanse on which to depict the scenes.

From 1933, Noke introduced a range of Toby Jugs, and character jugs of all kinds became popular at Doulton's from then on.

A significant amount of tableware was produced, of course, and the opening of the new china works for domestic tableware in 1907 set the scene for Doulton's expansion into this sector of the business.

Doulton's venture into the art deco style was somewhat restrained, but during the 1930's a few deco ranges were produced. *Viridian* was a colourful ornamental range of vases and bowls; and, although the tablewares have not been closely examined in this survey, it is worth noting the *Radio* line in tableware (1935), which, according to the advertisement of the time was as 'fragile in motif as century old Chintz'.

## Collecting Doulton Pottery

Doulton were by far the largest producers of art pottery in this country. They built up a strong reputation for quality and artistry, such that although the range of products was extensive, each bears a characteristic that unmistakably says that it was made at Doulton. One can therefore instinctively recognise a Doulton piece, whatever the period, and since nearly all the wares are marked the collector need have little trouble with identification. However, the familiar 'Royal Doulton' mark used after 1902, poses a problem. It is still used today, and one has to closely analyse the style of a piece to discern its period of manufacture, especially since many fine and collectable items were made under this mark. On high quality art pieces the artist's mark is often of help, whilst some wares are actually dated.

The collector should be particularly wary of modern reproductions of earlier styles. Doulton are reproducing flambé wares, which closely resemble those of the 1920's. The only difference is in the freshness of appearance of the modern pieces, and the accompaniment of the title *Flambe* or similar. The modern pieces are nonetheless high quality products in their own right, but their value must be considerably less than their earlier, rarer counterparts.

Most Doulton antique pieces sell at a premium, in spite of the high output. This is because they are of good quality, and are readily available on the market.

Doulton were able to keep pace over the years with public demand and taste. The blue and brown wares with their rather heavy decoration were a product of the Victorian mood. Doulton's did not exert themselves generally to compete with the art nouveau trend of the 1890's, but readily catered for the decorative requirements of the Edwardian drawing-room. The 1920's and 1930's saw a surge of new ideas at Doulton which were the results of a concentrated resource of technical and artistic expertise. The Doulton collector therefore is presented with a very wide range of pieces from which to form a worthwhile and rewarding collection.

**References**

1) *'The Royal Doulton Story', by Paul Atterbury & Louise Irvine; pub. Royal Doulton Tableware Ltd., 1979.*

2) *'The Doulton Burslem Wares', by Desmond Eyles; pub. Barrie & Jenkins, 1980.*

3) *'The Doulton Lambeth Wares', by Desmond Eyles; pub. Hutchinson, 1975.*

4) *'Royal Doulton Figures Produced at Burslem 1890-1978', by Desmond Eyles & Richard Dennis; pub. Royal Doulton Tableware, 1978. (see Bibliography for new edition)*

5) *'Sir Henry Doulton', by Edmund Gosse; biography edited by Desmond Eyles; pub. Hutchinson, 1970.*

6) *'Royal Doulton Figures', by Louise Irvine; pub. Richard Dennis, 1981.*

7) *'Royal Doulton Series Ware', by Louise Irvine; pub. Richard Dennis, Vol. 1 1980, Vol. 2 1984, Vol. 3 1986, Vol. 4 1988.*

8) *'Doulton Flambé Animals', by Jocelyn Lukins; pub. privately, 1981.*

9) *'The Doulton Figure Collectors' Handbook', by Kevin Pearson; pub. Kevin Francis, 1986, 1988.*

10) *'The Lyle Price Guide to Doulton', by Mick Yeman; pub. Lyle Publications, 1987.*

11) *'Catalogue of an Exhibition of Doulton Stoneware & Terracotta 1870 - 1925', Part 1; pub. Richard Dennis, 1971.*

12) *'Doulton Pottery from the Lambeth & Burslem Studios 1873 - 1939', Part 2; pub. Richard Dennis, 1975.*

13) *'Doulton Ware & Products of Other British Potteries, the Woolley Collection Including "Lambeth Stoneware"', by Rhoda Edwards; catalogue published by London Borough of Lambeth, Directorate of Amenity Services, 1973.*

14) *'Hannah Barlow', catalogue of an exhibition at Christies, South Kensington, by Peter Rose; pub. Richard Dennis, 1985.*

15) *Royal Doulton 1815-1965, by Desmond Eyles; pub. Hutchinson, 1965.*

*Summary of the more familiar wares*

| | |
|---|---|
| All wares 1875-1890 | : characterised by rich colourings, modelling, carving, gilding, etc. |
| All wares 1890-1910 | : less carving; marbled efficts, glaze effects and 'new art' styles. |
| Brangwynware (from 1930) | : by Frank Brangwyn; sevaral patterns in mainly pastel pinks and greens on beige grounds; common. |
| Carrara Ware 1887-1896 | : white marble-like stoneware usually decorated in pastel colours; scarce. |
| Chang Ware (c.1927) | : by Charles J Noke; thick bodied ware with thickly congealed glazes and appliqué figures in flambé colours; mainly vases; rare. |
| Character wares (from c.1906) | : by Charles Noke; Toby Jugs, etc. |
| Chine Ware 1886-1914 | : impressed lace patterns on stoneware; also known as Slater's Patent; common. |
| Copper Lustre Ware 1887-1912 (Copper wares) | : jugs and candlesticks mainly, imitating copper. |
| Crown Lambeth Ware 1892-1900 | : fine textured earthenware with an ivory tint; rare. |
| Crystalline glazes c.1904-1914 | : by Cuthbert Bailey; scarce to rare. |
| Dickens Ware (from c.1906) | : scenes from Dickens' plays; transfer printed; uncommon. |
| Holbein Ware 1895-1914 | : by Charles J Noke; portraits of people in low relief by Walter Nunn and other artists. |
| Imitation Leather Wares 1890-1910 | : stoneware jugs and bottles imitating leather. |
| Impasto Ware 1879-1906 | : coloured slip decorated ware: common. |
| Leaf patterns 1886-1936 (Natural Foliage Ware) | : created by pressing real leaves into the wet clay, removing to expose pattern, and painting in browns and orange: common. |
| Marqueterie Ware 1886-1906 | : marquetry mosiac of coloured clays; rare. |
| Morrisian Ware 1901-1924 | : prints of Morris dancers and other figures: scarce. |
| Persian Ware 1884-1900 | : influenced by Wm. De Morgan; tiles and panels, mostly painted in blue, green, orange. (Revived from 1919 to 1922 for vases, bowls, plaques; all rare). |
| Rembrandt Ware 1898-1914 | : by Charles J Noke; landscapes in monotones of brown, orange or blue; mainly vases and jardinères decorated by Arthur Eaton and Walter Nunn; scarce. |
| Sang-de-boeuf and Rouge Flambé glazes from 1890 | : by Charles J Noke; general flambé made through the 1920's and revived during the 1970's. |
| Silicon Ware 1880-1912 | : a hard, smooth high-fired stoneware; jardinères, vases and flower-pots, easily recognised by its smooth beige coloured body, usually marked; common. |
| Sung Ware 1907-1925 | : by Charles J Noke; splashed and mottled effects in flambé colours; mainly vases; scarce. |
| Titanian Ware 1914-1929 | : mostly vases, plates and bowls in shades of blue with bird-of-paradise motif (common on a transfer-printed tableware design) or as a soft, eggshell-like glaze with birds in landscapes by artists such as Harry Allen and Edward Raby; also some figures; scarce. |
| Velluma Ware c.1912-1914 | : transfer-print decorations painted with soft colours of landscapes and figures in landscapes; rare. |

*Some of the Principal Artists*

|  |  |  |
|---|---|---|
| Eliza Banks | (at Doulton c.1876-c.1884) | - carved and foliate decoration |
| Arthur Barlow | ( " 1871-1876) | - leaf scroll decoration |
| Hannah B Barlow | ( " 1871-1913) | - sgraffito animals |
| Florence E Barlow | ( " 1873-1909) | - sgraffito birds and animals |
| Wilmot Brown | | - decorated flambé; landscape flambé |
| Frank A Butler | ( " 1872-1911) | - foliate designs and art nouveau |
| Mary Butterton | ( " c.1874-c.1894) | - flower painting (Lambeth) |
| Mary Capes | ( " c.1876-c.1883) | - flower painting (Lambeth) |
| Minna Crawley | ( " c.1877-c.1885) | - flower painting and Persian styles (Lambeth) |
| Arthur Eaton | | - decorated flambé |
| Emily J Edwards | ( " c.1872-c.1876) | - carved and foliate decoration |
| Louisa E Edwards | ( " c.1873-c.1890) | - carved and foliate decoration |
| John Eyre | ( " c.1884-c.1897) | - painted figures (Lambeth) |
| William Hodgkinson | | - decorated flambé |
| Francis Lee | ( " c.1875-c.1890) | - pâte-sur-pâte and foliate decoration |
| Esther Lewis | ( " c.1878-c.1895) | - painted figures in landscapes; mostly plates (Lambeth) |
| Florence Lewis | ( " c.1875-c.1897) | - painted flowers and birds on large vases; Carrara Ware (Lambeth |
| Edith Lupton | ( " c.1875-c.1896) | - pâte-sur-pâte and foliate decoration |
| John Henry McLellan | ( " c.1880-c.1910) | - tiles, murals, large vases and chargers with figures (Lambeth) |
| Mary Mitchell | ( " c.1874-c.1887) | - children |
| Fred Moore | | - decorated flambé |
| Harry Nixon | | - decorated flambé |
| William Parker | ( " c.1879-c.1892) | - intricate carving of foliate decoration |
| Edith Rogers | ( " c.1881-c.1884) | - detailed carving of foliate decoration |
| William Rowe | ( " c.1925 | - slip-cast and moulded figures, vases, plaques and plates. |
| Eliza Simmance | ( " 1873-1928 | - pâte-sur-pâte flowers; foliate decoration |
| Linnie Watt | ( " c.1876-c.1886) | - painted figures in landscapes; mostly plates (Lambeth) |
| Charles Yeomans | | - decorated flambé; landscape flambé |

*Some of the Principal Modellers*

|  |  |  |
|---|---|---|
| Harry Barnard | (at Doulton c1808-c.1890) | - dragons and grotesques |
| John Broad | ( " 1873-1919) | - stoneware figures 1912-1914 (eg. `The Bather' and 'Atlanta'); fountains and busts. |
| Richard Garbe (b.1876; d.1957) | ( " c.1931-c.1932) | - vases; busts; figures |
| Arthur Leslie Harradine | ( " 1902-1914) | - Dickens characters; stoneware spirit flasks of politicians; moulded figures |
| Mark V Marshall | ( " c.1876-c.1912) | - dragons and grotesques; art nouveau. |
| George Tinworth | ( " 1866-1913) | - animal studies; religious terra-cotta panels; salt-glaze stone-ware figurines; vases and jugs in floreate designs |

Artist's Marks (in monogram)

These are many and varied - below is a synopsis of the more important marks:-

Eliza S Banks

Arthur B Barlow

Florence E Barlow

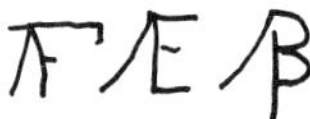

or

Hannah B Barlow

John Broad

Frank A Butler

Mary Capes

Minna L Crawley (faience)

Emily J Edwards

Arthur Leslie Harradine

*Some of the Principal Designers & Artist/Designers*

| | | |
|---|---|---|
| Frank A Butler | (at Doulton 1871-1911) | - vases, jugs, floreate designs |
| Frank Brangwyn | ( from late 1920's) | - tableware, vases, candlesticks, lamp-bases, plaques, etc. |
| Joan Cowper | ( " 1937-1939) | - vases, bowls (salt-glazed and unglazed) |
| Vera Huggins | ( " 1923-1950) | - salt-glaze stoneware pots from 1933-1935 |
| J H Mott | ( " c.1910-1929) | - crystalline and lustre glazes (one time art director at Lambeth) |
| Charles J Noke | ( " 1895-1936) | - flambé, sang-de-boeuf, crystalline glazes, face jugs (c.1920), etc. |
| Francis C Pope | ( " 1880-1923) | - slip-cast wares; gourd shapes |
| Edward Raby | ( " c.1901-1929) | - enamel colours, eg. Titanian Ware |
| Harry Simeon | ( " 1894-1936) | - figures, vases, plates; Persian Ware; Toby series ware |
| John Slater | (Art Director 1887-1914) | - Slater's Patent; Chine Ware, etc |
| Margaret E Thompson | (at Doulton c.1911-1925) | - female figures in art nouveau style on vases, plaques. |

**Factory Marks**

| | | | |
|---|---|---|---|
| Impressed: | DOULTON LAMBETH | | 1853 - c.1900 |
| ± name of ware | DOULTON LAMBETH | (within oval:<br>(within oval + year | c.1869-1872)<br>1872- 1879) |
| ± date | DOULTON LAMBETH | (written circular or within a circle | c.1887-1880) |
| ± artist's mark | DOULTON LAMBETH | (within rosette:<br>(+ 'England': | c.1879-1902<br>1891-1902) |
| ± Art Union of London | DOULTON LAMBETH ENGLAND | | 1891-c.1902 |
| | ROYAL DOULTON ENGLAND | (written circular, ± surmounted by a crown and lion) | 1902 -c.1922 |
| | ROYAL DOULTON ENGLAND | (written within a larger circle surrounded by lion only) | c.1922-1956 |
| | ROYAL DOULTON LAMBETH ENGLAND | (written vertically and semi oval) | c1912-1956 |

Agnette Hoy

AH

Vera Huggins

Edith D Lupton

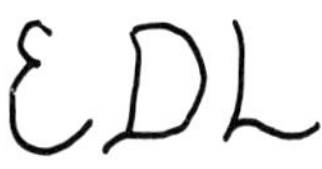

Mark V Marshall

Frank C Pope

F·C·P

William Rowe

Harry Simeon

Eliza Simmance

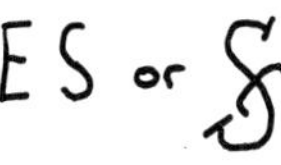

George Tinworth

Margaret E Thompson

# ELTON WARE

## By Sir Edmund Elton (artist/potter)
## Sunflower Pottery, Clevedon Court, Clevedon, Avon. (1881 - 1920)

Typical Wares: earthenware

### Historical Background

**In 1883, upon succeeding to the title of eighth baronet, Sir Edmund Elton and his wife took up residence in the family home of Clevedon Court, a splendid manor house dating from the 14th Century, situated near the Bristol Channel at Clevedon in Somerset.**

Sir Edmund had become interested in pottery making about the year 1880, and being of a highly inventive nature decided to learn all he could about the complex art of ceramics. By 1884, and after many exhausting attempts at kiln design, glaze recipes and clay firing, he believed he had developed 'a sound and marketable ware' such that he was able, with the help of two servant assistants (George Masters and Charlie Neads), to establish his *Sunflower Pottery* in the grounds of Clevedon Court.

Sir Edmund had a firm belief in the value of the crafts. He frequently showed pieces at international exhibitions, but never undertook any serious business venture for his pottery, and, although pieces were sold at prestigious establishments such as Tiffany's in New York, many were given away as presents.

Being an accomplished water-colourist, Sir Edmund was able to produce some spectacular floral designs for his pots, often drawn from specimens in his own greenhouses. He was able to adapt his designs readily to the shape of a pot, creating a symmetry which only the combination of artist and engineer could accomplish.

Until 1902, the output of the Sunflower Pottery consisted entirely of slip-decorated earthenware. From 1902, Sir Edmund began experimenting with liquid gold and platinum, producing metallic glazes which were coated on to pieces over a coloured primary glaze and which crazed during firing. The *craquele-ware*, as Sir Edmund called it, achieved international success.

Sir Edmund also produced items of Church furniture in Elton ware, not only in slip-ware but also in crackle ware. These ecclesiastical pieces are still to be found in some churches today, and consist mostly of candlesticks, crosses and religious plaques.

Sir Edmund died in 1920, and his son, Sir Ambrose Elton, tried to carry on the Pottery. George Masters, however, (Sir Edmund's premier assistant) died in 1922, and without his skill, Sir Ambrose found it difficult to continue beyond this date.

### Products

Output was mainly in the form of vases and jugs, but there were also tygs (three-handled loving cups) teapots (of extraordinary complexity), bowls, ewers, tobacco-jars, candlesticks, plates (rare), jardineres (rare) and plaques (scarce).

Shapes were either simple or highly complex, and relief moulding or bossing were common. Stylised floral motifs in relief were the most common form of decoration, and the sunflower was a favourite Elton subject, particularly the seed-heads which he often expressed as a series of raised dots, either geometrically or randomly scattered.

The earliest wares produced were crude in shape and decoration. Later on, Sir Edmund became influenced by early South American styles, and also styles from the Mediterranean, Africa and the Orient. Exotic handles, contorted spouts, squashed rims and ovoid bodies are common expressions of these many influences.

The cracklewares were generally less highly embellished with surface decoration, relying more on the lustrous effect of the glazes for attraction. Sometimes, the gold crackle appears as a copper colour, the firing producing subtle variants. All the crackle wares show the primary glaze colour through the cracks. This colour is usually yellow, green or blue.

*Group of crackle wares, gold and platinum crackle. (tall vase, centre, 230 mm high).*

The collector will doubtless come across several commemorative items, such as 'Kitchener' mugs, wares commemorating the Jubilees of Queen Victoria and King Edward VII, and wares celebrating the end of the First World War (inscribed 'Pax 1918'). There were also some special commemorations.

## Collecting Elton Ware

Elton Ware is easily recognised by the collector. The highly polished effect of the glazes and the ubiquitous floral motifs are strong indicators.

Pieces are keenly sought after, and like De Morgan's pottery, have an important place in the history of ceramics. Some pieces are very fine and demand high prices, especially those with metallic glazes and large pieces. Generally though, Elton Ware is still somewhat under-collected in comparison to other pottery of its class.

## Marks

Generally, all pieces are marked. The presence of the year or date is rare. Marks prior to 1884 are varied. A single painted sunflower has been noted on a vase without the name Elton. From 1920 to 1922, the signature 'Elton' is accompanied by a cross, signifying pieces decorated after Sir Edmund Elton's death.

On the base of each piece are three unglazed marks left by the clay supports of the kiln (ref. also Pilkington Pottery for similar marks), which exhibit the red earthenware body below the glaze. Pieces with a totally glazed base are scarce, and pieces with totally unglazed bases are probably from Sir Edmund's very early kilns, and so very rare. Pieces with a white earthenware body are extremely rare, and are representative of Sir Edmund's experiments using other than local clay materials.

Pieces comprising more than one part, such as a vase and cover, are usually marked with a matching letter or number (either painted or on a paper label).

**References**

*1) See the spectacular collection at Clevedon Court, open through the National Trust. The collection is in the Tea-Room, and the Court is situated close to the Clevedon exit of the M5 Motorway.*

*2) Pieces are also on display at the Victoria Art Gallery, Bath, the Reference Library and Guildhall, Bath, and also at Somerset County Museum, Taunton Castle, Taunton. Reading Museum boasts an extensive collection. The V & A in Kensington also have a few pieces on show, as do Exeter Museum, which have some pieces currently on loan to Country houses, such as Knightshayes Court, Tiverton. Sir Edmund Elton made several bequests to Museums throughout the country.*

*3) Note the Clock Tower in Clevedon's 'Triangle' (the centre of the old village) which has Elton pottery panels, and also Tickenham Church closeby (permission to visit required), which boasts an altar on Elton Ware columns as well as other pieces.*

*4) "Elton Ware - The Pottery of Sir Edmund Elton", by Malcolm Haslam; pub. Richard Dennis, 1989.*

*5) "Elton Ware Rediscovered" by the author, Antique Collector Magazine, July 1985.*

*6) "Elton Ware - The Genius of Sir Edmund Elton, Potter- Baronet", by the author; The Antique Collectors' Club magazine, Vol. 21, No. 9, Feb. 1987.*

*7) "Elton Ware", by the author; Bristol Illustrated magazine; Nov. 1986.*

*8) "Eltonware at Clevedon Court", by Julia Elton; National Trust magazine, 1980.*

*9) "A Victorian Squire & His Eccentric Pottery"; article by Pamela Ruck in Art & Antiques, March 27, 1976.*

*10) "Elton Ware"; article by Cosmo Monkhouse in The Magazine of Art, 1882.*

| Type of Ware | Production | Quality | Availability |
|---|---|---|---|
| Earthenware 1881-4: | Very Low | Poor | Scarce |
| Elton Ware:- (1884-1920) Slip-ware | Medium | Good to Very Good | Uncommon |
| Metallic glazes: | Low to Medium | Good to Excellent | Scarce |
| Combined metallic & slip-ware | Very Low | Excellent | Very rare |
| Ecclesiastical ware | Low | Poor to Very Good | Rare |
| Commemoratives | Low | Poor to Very Good | Scarce |

| | | |
|---|---|---|
| Painted in black or blue: | E.H. Elton Clevedon | (1881-4) |
| (and variants) | Elton Clevedon | (1881-4) |
| Incised: | E | (1881-4) |
| Impressed: | ••ELTON•• | (1884-1920) |
| Painted signature in black or blue: | Elton | (1884-1920) |
| | ℇ (generally on smaller pieces) | (1884-1920) |
| ±year | E (generally on smaller pieces) | (1884-1920) |
| | Elton (plus a cross) | (1920-1922) |

# FARNHAM POTTERY

## Farnham, Surrey (1873 - present)

Typical Wares: red clay wares, art pottery from 1880

### Historical Background

**In 1873, Absalom Harris set up a pottery at Clay Hill, Wreccelsham, near Farnham, having previously had a pottery at Charles Hill, Elstead (1860-1866) and also in Alice Holt Forest (1866-1872). The local deposits of Gault Clay were utilised, and red clay wares were produced, consisting of drain-pipes, tiles, plant pots, chimney pots and other domestic items.**

After 1880, however, a different type of ware began to be produced which became known as *Farnham Greenware*. The name *Greenware* was derived from the lead glaze used, which was made green by the use of copper oxide.

The ware developed through requests for copies of medieval and Roman pieces, which sprang from an initial request by the artist Birket Foster (who lived nearby) to have a badly weathered garden vase copied.

Absalom Harris became quite adept at producing copies of earlier pottery styles, and freely imitated Tudor and Roman pieces. He also copied the styles of Brannam's *Barum Ware*, such as Brannam's cat bowl.

The trade in copies grew and through the many commissions received became quite profitable in relation to the ordinary work of producing red plant-pots.

From 1880 until 1939, art pottery at Farnham was made in conjunction with Farnham School of Art, where art pieces were exhibited by Harris in 1890. The local artist W H Allen was instrumental in establishing the connection with Farnham School of Art (where he was Art Master) and also for providing designs from his students. The students' designs were executed by the potters and the resultant pots were returned to the students for decoration prior to being fired - a co-operation which proved beneficial both for the school and for the pottery.

From 1892, pieces were retailed through Heals and Liberty, a practice which continued through the 1920's.

The publicity brought by the *Greenwares* enhanced the reputation of the pottery, and additional buildings had to be erected. The domestic and horticultural side of the business also expanded, and the workforce was increased.

Absalom's two sons and two daughters became involved with the running of the pottery, as well as producing pieces in their own right.

The two World Wars caused the inevitable down-turn in business, but the pottery survived. With the fall in demand for Art Pottery during the 1940's, the pottery survived on the production of its horticultural wares.

The pottery continues today, still under the management of the Harris family.

### Products

Most pieces were decorated in a single green glaze, with little or no pattern on simple shapes; but after 1914 brighter glazes were introduced in colours such as yellow and blue (although still generally monochrome). Some simple decoration in black, such as a zig-zag frieze, occasionally accompanied the green glazes. The words 'yellow' and 'green' are often to be found incised on the base of

*Selection of 'Green Wares'. l to r:- i) vase, 230 mm high, marked 'Green' on base, dated 1929. ii) ewer, 325 mm high. iii) two- handled vase, 203 mm high. (courtesy HCMS, ACM 1957.63/2; ACM 1936.89/7; ACM 1936.89/3).*

pieces, as if there is any doubt about the colour of the glaze!

Many designs were taken from pieces in the Victoria & Albert Museum, and included Medieval and Roman styles; others were supplied by students at the Farnham School of Art. Owl pitchers, amphora and 'rustic fern pots' were regular designs, but pitchers and vases of many shapes were produced.

From 1905, some sgraffito designs were produced, and during the 1920's Barbra Daysh created geometric sgraffito patterns at the Farnham School of Art, as well as copies of Spanish and Moorish styles.

The sgraffito designs were often effected on a cream glaze ground, and the red earthenware body frequently shows through the glaze. Patterns tended to be much more decorative and intricate than anything executed on the 'greenwares', and some large chargers seem to have provided a suitable vehicle for some spectacular work.

Agnes Hall, who was assistant Art Mistress at Farnham School of Art during the 1920's, also used the sgraffito technique to produce some pieces in an art deco style.

W H Allen was associated with the pottery from 1889 to 1943. Apart from designing the more general *'greenware'* he worked with William Freemantle Harris (one of Absalom's sons) to produce press-moulded birds, animals and architectural wares. The modelled pieces bear some resemblance to the work of the Martin Brothers.

Absalom's daughters, Gertrude and Nellie Harris, also worked in the pottery, and undertook both architectural and *'greenware'* work.

Another significant artist at Farnham School of Art was Ada K Hazell (c.1897/8) who is recorded as having sold pieces at Heals and Liberty under the name of 'Farnham Sgraffito Pottery'.

The more decorative pieces are usually marked, but the planer *'greenwares'* are often to be found unmarked. As an aid to identification, Farnham wares exhibit a particular iridescence of glaze, owing to the high lead content. The iridescence is particularly noticeable on the base of the *'greenwares'*.

***References***

*1) 'Farnham Pottery', by P.C.D. Brears, pub. Phillimore & Co Ltd. 1971*

*2) The Farnham Pottery, Pottery Lane, Wrecclesham. Tel. Farnham 715318*

*3) The Curtis- Allen Gallery, Alton, has a good representative display, which includes a bequest of pieces from W H Allen. W H Allen's sketchbooks are housed in the collections of Hampshire County Museums Service at Chilcomb House, Chilcomb Lane, Winchester.*

*Owl jug, 157 mm high, blue glaze. (courtesy HCMS, ACM 1936.89/6).*

| **Type of Ware** | **Production** | **Quality** | **Availability** |
|---|---|---|---|
| Garden ornaments and large items | Moderate | Poor to Good | Common (but difficult to identify) |
| Art wares | Low to Moderate | Fair to Very Good | Uncommon (highly decorative pieces rare) |

**Marks**

Many pieces are unmarked, but noted marks are:-

F.S.P. Farnham Sgraffito Pottery

HARRIS<br>HAND MADE<br>FARNHAM<br>SURREY<br>ENGLAND (enclosed in a square)

(figure of an owl)

± artists' marks

e.g. B Barbra Daysh

± 'yellow' or 'green' incised

# THE FOLEY POTTERIES

## Wileman & Co (1872-1925)
## Shelley Potteries Ltd., Fenton/Longton, Staffs. (1925-1966)

Typical wares: earthenwares, lustres, bone china

## Historical Background

**The Foley Potteries, named after a local family, were set up by John Smith of Fenton Hall around 1827. Blue printed earthenwares and plain white china were manufactured until 1872, when the potteries were taken over by James F. Wileman in partnership with Joseph Shelley, and known as 'Wileman & Co.'.**

When Joseph Shelley's son Percy joined the business in 1881 he began to improve designs and increase business. Reports of 1893 talk of an expanding trade in rich and varied tea-sets and table decorations, inspite of a somewhat depressed market. Showrooms were established in London together with agencies in Australia, Canada and the USA.

When Joseph Shelley died in 1896, Percy Shelley took over and set about recruiting reputable artists, such as Rowland Morris, who designed one of the most successful wares of the pottery - the *Dainty White* range of tea-ware. Production of this ware continued through to 1966 when the factory closed. Morris's untimely death in 1898 was thus a significant loss to the pottery.

The well known designer Frederick Rhead joined Wileman as art director about 1897, and was influential in creating new pottery lines such as sgraffito decorated pieces in coloured parian ware and a large range of painted underglaze wares.

Many of Rhead's new lines were given Italianate names, the most popular of which was *Intarsio*, although this name referred only to a style and not to a particular pattern or motif. Other ranges were *Urbato, Faience, Primitif, Pastello* and *Spano-Lustra.*

*Charger, 300 mm. diam., blue and yellow lustre with gilding, marked 'Shelley England'.*

In 1905, Walter Slater (of Doulton) took over as art director, and Frederick Rhead left to concentrate on writing, illustrating and other design work. Rhead went on to become art director of Wood & Sons in 1912, a position which lasted until 1929, during which time he wrote many articles on pottery and became highly respected throughout the trade. He died in 1933.

In 1910, the name 'Shelley China' was promoted because of a conflict with other potteries using the name 'Foley China' (ref E Brain & Co.)

Wileman & Co. exhibited at the British Industries Fair at Crystal Palace in 1920 and also at the British Industrial Arts Exhibition in Knightsbridge the same year. A few Shelley pieces were shown at both exhibitions, which subsequently proved successful.

The Shelley range became so successful that a separate company was set up in 1925 as Shelley Potteries Ltd.. Prior to this date most of Wileman's wares were marked 'Foley Art China'.

The company went from strength to strength. Percy Shelley's two sons had entered the business before the Great War and continued to expand production into the 1920's.

In 1925 the employment of the illustrator Hilda Cowham heralded the launch of a highly successful venture into nursery ware under the name *Playtime*. A year later, the illustrator Mabel Lucie Attwell was engaged. She designed extensive ranges of nursery wares for Shelley in all shapes and styles.

The popularity of these wares brought competition from other potteries such as Doulton, who launched their *Bunnykins* range from 1934. Equally popular, however, were the Shelley jelly moulds, of which more than 50 shapes were produced in thick white china until 1939.

Percy Shelley retired from the business in 1932, and by 1938 Walter Slater had also retired. The company lasted until 1966, however, when it was taken over by Allied English Potteries (now part of the Doulton Group).

### Products

The Intarsio range includes many genre studies, such as characters from plays by Shakespeare, as well as animals and birds (cats, geese and peacocks, for example). Decoration was accomplished by painting onto transfer prints underglaze. The colours were bold and bright, often being painted against a brown background. The pieces exhibit many influences of which one of the most recognisable is a Dutch approach to shape and decoration.

Urbato items were tube-line decorated, whilst Spano-Lustra was characterised by a lustrous glaze over sgraffito decoration. The Pastello range was similar to Intarsio, though recognisable by the use of pastel colours over a dark ground, and the Faience range featured decoration by the use of coloured slips.

Some grotesques were also made, mostly animals and mythical beasts. In 1911, a new range of Intarsio ware was introduced. This was followed by numerous other new ranges, some of which adapted well to the increased demand for toilet sets - *Etruscan, Alexandra, Cloisello*, etc., were some of the patterns which appeared as jug and basin sets.

From about 1913, bone china was also produced, much of which appeared under the Shelley mark. From 1915, Wileman & Co. introduced some interesting ranges entitled *Roself, Violette, Roumana, Rosata* and *Vinta*, all of which were exhibited at their London showroom. The designs were classically inspired, with vivid colourings, many having lustre and gilt finishes, and occurred as tea-sets, floating flower bowls, spill vases, plates and other articles.

During the early 1920's the commemorative and souvenir trade proved particularly lucrative, and various moulded miniatures were produced with heraldic motifs, from cars, boats and trains to shaving mugs and comical animals.

The first real art pottery to be produced at Wileman & Co. after the Great War appeared from 1920 as Shelley lustre ware. Initial experiments, however, produced poor quality lustres, but the technique was soon perfected. The Oriental influence is particularly noticeable in these wares.

The 1930's saw new ranges of tea- sets in typical art deco style. The *Mode* (1930), *Vogue* (1930) and *Eve* (1934) shapes were characterised by triangular handles, and appeared in a variety of bright deco patterns such as *Sunray* and *Butterfly Wing*. The *Regent* shape was characterised by circular handles, and also appeared in deco patterns.

In 1932, Shelley launched *Harmony Artware*, which was a range of high-fired wares, characterised by streaks of bold colours, mainly bichromes of purple, green, orange or pink. The effect was produced by mixing turpentine with the glaze and spinning the pots on the wheel while the glaze was still wet. *Harmony Artware* was very popular and produced in great quantity.

Some of the Shelley lustrewares are popular with collectors, commanding high prices at auction. The appeal is in the rich decoration and attractive colour combinations. Designs included stylised animals and birds, butterflies and other insects, and the pieces are comparable to the Wedgwood lustres in quality.

**References**


*1) Frederick & George Rhead's book 'Staffordshire Pots & Potters'; pub. Hutchinson & Co. 1906 (reprinted by EP Publishing, 1977)*
*2) 'Shelley Potteries, The History & Production of a Staffordshire Family of Potters', by Chris Watkins, William Harvey & Robert Senft; pub. Barrie & Jenkins, 1986.*
*3) 'Mabel Lucie Attwell'; catalogue of a centenary exhibition at Brighton Museum, 1979, by A Packer.*
*4) 'Shelley Potteries'; catalogue of an exhibition at the Geffrye Museum, 1980.*


| Type of Ware | Production | Quality | Availability |
|---|---|---|---|
| Named wares by Frederick Rhead | Low to High | Fair to Very Good | Common (except Urbato and Spano-Lustra which are scarce, and Primitif and Pastello which are rare) |
| Other wares pre-Shelley | Moderate to High | Fair to Good | Abundant |
| Shelley wares (non lustres) | High | Fair to Good | Abundant |
| Shelley lustres | Low to moderate | Poor (early) to Excellent | Uncommon (high quality) |

**Marks**
Printed:

|  |  |
|---|---|
| W & Co. (in monogran surmounted by a crown) | 1872-1890 |
| THE FOLEY (as above) W & Co. | 1890-1910 |
| THE FOLEY CHINA ENGLAND | c.1872 - c.1920 |
| FOLEY ART CHINA | c.1920 - 1925 |
| SHELLEY ENGLAND (in capitals in shield) | c.1912 - 1925 |
| Shelley England (in signature in shield) | 1925 - 1940 |
| Shelley CHINA ENGLAND | 1930 - 1932 |

± 'FINE BONE CHINA' (1945 - 1966)
± ware name
± pattern number
± registered design number

# THE FOLEY POTTERY

## E. Brain & Co. Fenton, Staffs. (1903 - 1967)

Typical Wares : earthenwares, bone-china

### Historical Background & Products

**The Foley Pottery was run by Robinson & Son from 1881, but in 1903 came under the operation of E. Brain & Co. It was situated just across the road from Wileman & Co., and used the name 'Foley' along with many other potteries nearby. In fact Brain objected to Percy Shelley's attempt in 1910 to register the name 'Foley China' at Wileman & Co. A resulting court case decided that Wileman & Co. had no exclusive right to the name 'Foley China'.**

Wares produced at Brain & Co. were noted for their simplicity of design, with neat individual lines of decoration. The pottery body was heavy and hard-wearing, all pieces having a characteristically curved interior base to avoid dirt collecting.

Mostly domestic wares were produced in bone-china, such as tea and breakfast sets, but from 1905 a range of *Peacock Pottery* was produced which was well received in the trade. Small giftwares were also made, as a response to a growing souvenir trade.

In 1920, E Brain & Co. were exhibitors at the British Industrial Arts Exhibition, and during the 1930's much work was produced in association with the Royal Staffordshire Pottery of A J Wilkinson Ltd., some of which was exhibited at the Harrods Tableware Exhibition in 1934.

Brain & Co. produced their contribution to the many ranges of art deco tea-sets during the 1930's, and their *Foley Mayfair* (1932) range was similar in style to Shelley's *Vogue* and *Mode* ranges. Some tea-sets were also produced in a cubist style, with square cups and tea- pots. Decoration was fairly restrained, however, and styles such as *Cubist Landscape* and *Cubist Sunflower* featured decoration only on part of a piece, such as the rim.

In 1930, the strongly curved *Pallas* shape was launched for tableware, and was decorated in a variety of deco styles. More traditional shapes were also made in the 1930's, and *Devon*, *Perth* and *Avon* typically carried floral scenes. A successful design was *Clovelly*, using blue, green, yellow and pink colours.

In 1932, Thomas Fennemore joined Brain & Co. as Managing Director, bringing with him previous sales skills in the pottery industry. With his appointment, Brain & Co. increased their ranges by launching new designs specifically aimed at mass- production.

In 1933, Brain & Co. launched six designs for tea- ware with floral motifs in a conical shape with angled handles called *Langham*. Again, this shape was similar to Shelley's *Regent*, but was characterised by the handles containing the outline shape of a diamond. In the same year, a polka-dot range was produced for the mass-market called simply *Spot*, again similar to Shelley's.

Work was also commissioned by Fennemore from contemporary artists, such as Vanessa Bell, Frank Brangwyn, Gordon Forsyth, Laura Knight, Graham Sutherland, Clarice Cliff and Fanny Rhead (who was known to have submitted a series of twelve Egyptian designs). The association of such well- known artists with mass-produced wares seems ironic, but, as it happens, their work sold at a premium and was quickly snapped up by discerning collectors.

E. Brain & Co. acquired the Coalport Company in 1958, and became part of the Wedgwood Group in 1967.

*Teapot, 100 mm high, design attributed to the Glaswegian artist George Logan.*

| **Type of Ware** | **Production** | **Quality** | **Availability** |
|---|---|---|---|
| All Wares | High | Fair to Good | Abundant |

**Marks**

| Printed: | Mark | Date |
|---|---|---|
| | E B & CO<br>F. | 1903 - ? |
| | ESTABLISHED<br>E B & CO ) in rope<br>F. ) motif<br>FOLEY CHINA | 1903 - ? |
| | FOLEY<br>E B & CO<br>CHINA<br>ENGLISH BONE CHINA | 1930 - 1936 |

± artist's signature

± ware name, eg 'Peacock Pottery' printed within a peacock picture.

# GRANVILLE POTTERY

## Hanley, Stoke-on-Trent (1895 - 1898)

Typical Wares: hollow wares, plates & dishes

### Historical Background

**The Granville Pottery was founded in 1895 by the Italian sculptor Carlo Manzoni (b.1885- 1910). Manzoni was a gentleman of private means, who was skilled in anatomy, languages, sculpture, mosaics and wood-carving. It seems that he maintained close contact with Harold Rathbone and Conrad Dressler, the co-directors of the Della Robbia Pottery, so much so that when Dressler left Della Robbia, Manzoni closed his own pottery and joined Rathbone (see Della Robbia). Manzoni died in 1910.**

### Products

Vases, jugs, plates and dishes were the main output of the Granville Pottery, strongly influenced in design by the Italian Renaissance period. The pieces are similar to those produced by Manzoni at Della Robbia, with incised and painted decoration on a red pottery body, but in a much cruder form.

The painting and glazes are fairly thick, and easily damaged if knocked. (Care should be taken with cleaning, as for Della Robbia). The colours employed were less subtle than at Della Robbia (though even these can be quite vivid), and more gaudy in appearance - bright green, red-brown and yellow frequently occurring together on a piece.

The majority of designs were geometric patterns, floriate in style. Painted scenes are extremely rare.

**References**

*1) Victoria & Albert Museum, London.*

*Two pieces by Carlo Manzoni. l to r:- i) jug, 134 mm high, ii) bottle vase, 190 mm high.*

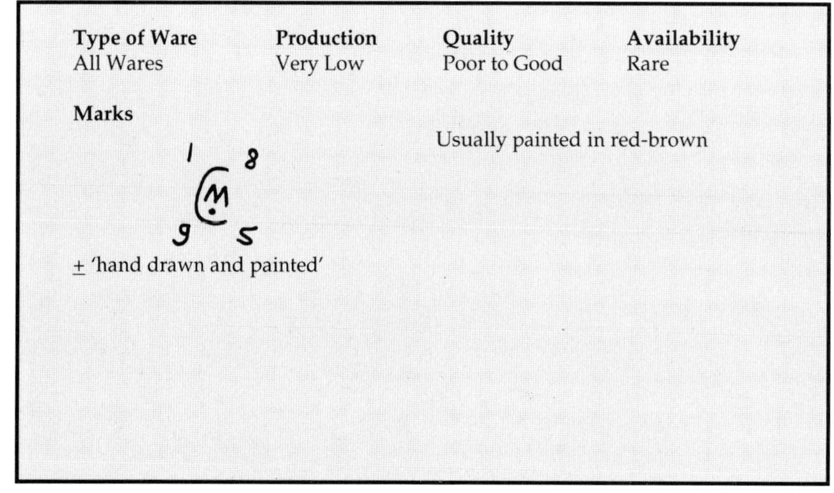

| Type of Ware | Production | Quality | Availability |
|---|---|---|---|
| All Wares | Very Low | Poor to Good | Rare |

**Marks**



Usually painted in red-brown

± 'hand drawn and painted'

# A E GRAY LTD (1907-1961)

## Glebe Works, Hanley, Staffs. (1907-1933)
## Whieldon Road, Stoke-on-Trent (1934-1961)

Typical Wares: porcelain, earthenware, stoneware, lustres

### Historical Background

**A E Gray established his business as a decorating studio in 1907, having previously been a glass and china salesman in a Manchester retail shop.**

During the 1920's, A E Gray Ltd., were producing fine art vases, jugs and bowls in stoneware, with sgrafitto decorations. Gray was conscious of the demand for colourful hand-painted pottery and employed quality designers at his studio. The studio was only a decorating enterprise, however, and all the wares were brought in from other potteries as undecorated white-ware, much of it coming from Johnson Brothers.

In 1922, the designer Susie Cooper (b.1903) was taken on from the Burslem School of Art, where she had studied under the artist Gordon Forsyth (ref. Pilkinton Pottery). She was paid on a 'time work' basis and given free rein to create her own designs.

In 1929, Susie Cooper left Gray to set up on her own, and for a short period she had a studio at the Chelsea Works in Burslem. From 1932, however, she was designing tableware for her own Company in premises offered to her by H Wood & Sons, an arrangement which gave her the opportunity to control the shape of her pieces as well as the decoration.

Her early work was exhibited at the British Empire Exhibition in 1924, and in Paris in 1925. Later designs were shown regularly at the British Industries Fair from 1932, and at the Festival of Britain in 1951. She was awarded the OBE in 1979.

The Crown Works merged with the Royal Tuscan China Company in 1961, and this Company became part of the Wedgwood Group in 1966. Susie Cooper continues to design today on a freelance basis. After 1961, A E Gray Ltd also became part of the Wedgwood Group.

**SUSIE COOPER**

**1922-1929 at Gray's**

**1930-1931 at Chelsea Works, Burslem**

**1932-1961 at Crown Works, Burslem**

### Products

The early Gray's wares were hand-painted. Designs by Susie Cooper at A E Gray Ltd were initially heavily floral or as bright geometric bands. She also produced several high quality pieces in silver or copper lustres as tea-sets and other tableware. These lustres were generically known as *Gloria Lustre*, and were developed in collaboration with Gordon Forsyth.

Lustre patterns were mostly geometric with foliage, and were later reproduced in lustre on porcelain from 1930 to 1933.

Susie Cooper's non-lustre pieces at A E Gray Ltd often contained bright colours of orange, brown or green, but during the 1930's her colours became more pastel and the patterns smaller and more delicate.

Small floral motifs on tableware were popular, as was a running deer pattern. More deco styles included simple concentric lines of a single colour, as in the *Crayon Lines* pattern, executed on rounded deco shapes. *Kestrel* (1931) and *Curlew* (1935) were typical of these shapes. Pastel green, grey and brown were predominant colours used by Susie Cooper during the 1930's.

*Coffee-set in 'Kestrel' shape, Crown Works, Burslem.*

Painted decoration gave way to experimental lithographic decoration on Susie Cooper's wares from 1935 to 1939. *Dresden Spray* was a particularly successful lithographed pattern, but there were several hundred others.

From 1936, a range of nurseryware was produced by Susie Cooper, exploiting the market opened by Shelley with their Mabel Lucie Attwell ranges. About this time some sgrafitto decorated ware was also produced by Susie Cooper.

The art ware of A E Gray Ltd is very attractive but much under- collected. The lack of individual items (ie not as sets) probably has much to do with this. The porcelain tea-sets are English in style, but the decoration is very much of the Eastern Mediterranean, reflecting a certain warmth of design even though metallic lustres were often used. 'V'-shaped wall vases were popular items during the 1930's, and appeared in a variety of sizes with soft deco foliate designs in yellow and orange colours, often gilded. These and similar deco style wares from A E Gray Ltd are particularly popular with collectors.

**Reference**

*1) 'Hand Painted Gray's Pottery'; pub. City Museum & Art Gallery, Stoke-on-Trent, 1982, 1983, new edition 1987.*

*2) 'Elegance & Utility 1924-1978: The Work of Susie Cooper, A Tribute from Wedgwood'; catalogue by Adrian Woodhouse of an Exhibition at Sanderson's Showrooms, London, 1978.*

*3) 'Susie Cooper Productions'; catalogue by Ann Eatwell of an Exhibition at the Victoria & Albert Museum, London and the City Museum & Art Gallery, Stoke-on-Trent, 1987.*

*4) 'Susie Cooper - Pride of the Potteries'; article by Graham Crossingham-Gower in Art & Antiques, April 12, 1975.*

*5) 'A Bold Experiment in Tableware Design'(1934 Harrods Exhibition); article by Ann Eatwell in the journal of the Antique Collectors' Club, November 1984.*

*6) 'Sixty Glorious Years - The Work of Susie Cooper, OBE'; article by Neil Fletcher in the journal of the Antique Collectors' Club, October, 1984.*

*7) 'Excellent in its Simplicity' (Susie Cooper); article by C Haig McDonald in The Antique Collector, July, 1987.*

*8) 'In the Advance Spirit' (Susie Cooper); article by Graham Peake in The Antique Dealer & Collector, July, 1987.*

*9) 'Susie Cooper, Diverse Designer'; article by Su Snodin in The Antique Collector, August, 1982.*

*10) 'As Fresh as 50 Years Ago' (Susie Cooper); article by Victor Winstone in Art & Antiques, June 10, 1978.*

| **Type of Ware** | **Production** | **Quality** | **Availability** |
|---|---|---|---|
| Designs by Susie Cooper | Moderate to High | Good to Very Good | Common |

**Marks**

1) **A E Gray Ltd.**

| | | | |
|---|---|---|---|
| Transfer Printed: | (galleon on water plus legend 'A E Gray & Co Ltd Hanley England') | | 1912-1930 |
| ± 'Designed by Susie Cooper' or 'Susie Cooper Ware' | | | 1925-1929 |
| ± artist's signature (Susie Cooper)<br>(NB: from 1930, Susie Cooper worked for herself) | | | |
| Transfer Printed: | (galleon on water plus legend: 'Hand Painted Gray's Pottery Hanley England' in square frame or square outline) | | 1930-1933 |
| | (galleon on water plus three wavy lines) | | 1934-1961 |
| ± 'Hand Painted'<br>± 'England' | | | |

2) **Susie Cooper** (1930-1961)

| | | | |
|---|---|---|---|
| Stamped: | A<br>SUSIE<br>COOPER<br>PRODUCTION | (in black triangle) | 1930-1931 |
| Transfer overglaze: | A<br>SUSIE COOPER<br>PRODUCTION<br>CROWN WORKS<br>BURSLEM<br>ENGLAND | (surmounted by a leaping deer) | 1932-1939 |
| | Susie Cooper<br>England | | 1952-1953 |
| ± pattern name and number | | | |

# ISLE OF WIGHT HANDCRAFT POTTERY

## Gunville, Carisbrooke, Newport, Isle of Wight. (1926-1938)

Typical Wares: earthenwares

### Historical Background

**Samuel Edgar Saunders established his Isle of Wight Handcraft Pottery in 1926 at Gunville, Carisbrooke, having obtained a brickworks from Pritchett & Co. about 1920.**

The 'Charisbrooke Brick, Tile & Pottery Works' had a Head Office and Showrooms at 110, High Street, Newport, Isle of Wight, but hand-made pottery was advertised as Isle of Wight Handcraft Pottery.

Apparently the Brickworks Manager, Frederick Joseph Mursell was impressed by the suitability of clays on the island for ceramics, and suggested the making of glazed pottery.

The clay utilised was a red clay from Afton in the west of the island, and the kilns used were modelled on kilns at the Ceramic Works in Devres, France.

Mursell visited the Staffordshire Potteries and took on a potter by the name of Laye to supervise the establishment of the Handcraft Pottery. It seems that several people were employed in the making of Isle of Wight Handcraft wares. It is recorded that in 1930 Mr Laye was in charge of glazing, and a potter from Stafford by the name of Jackson was in charge of potting, whilst the painter and designer was a Mr Reg Davies. The manager of the pottery at this time was Edward Jervison Bagley, who had sole charge of the operation.

A great variety of shapes and patterns was created, and because each piece was hand-made no two pieces appeared exactly alike, although many bore a similar decorative motif. "The keynote...[was]... simplicity and grace of outline combined with softness of colour", exclaimed the first catalogue of wares.

Pieces were stated to have been purchased by Queen Mary, and Princess Beatrice was said to have taken a keen interest in the pottery. A London Showroom is recorded as having been at 15, Gamage Buildings in the 'pottery mecca' of Holborn, E.C.1; but in spite of any prestige by this outlet or Royal patronage, the pottery never made a profit, and according to a newspaper report of 1938, the enterprise was carried on more 'out of sentiment, fulfilling a useful purpose on the island'.

Samuel Saunders lived at Padmore House in Whippingham, Isle of Wight, but there is little information at present as to his involvement in the pottery. He also owned the firm of Saunders Ltd., boat builders and seaplane manufacturers, which was also based on the island (later becoming Saunders-Rowe Aviation).

Samuel Saunders died in 1933, and ownership of the pottery passed to his son, Hulbert Samuel Saunders. In 1938, the Pottery Manager, Edward Bagley, was found guilty of theft, through making and selling ceramic roundels without Hulbert Saunders' knowledge or consent. As a result of this case, and because he had no knowledge of the intricacies of pottery making, Hulbert Saunders decided to close the Handcraft Pottery. The Brickworks, however, continued for some time afterwards.

### Products

Mostly vases were produced, sometimes two-handled, of smallish stature and simple shape (the tallest being 375 mm high), but other wares included bowls, plates, candlesticks, jugs, egg-cups, lamp-bases, lemonade sets, tea and coffee sets, jars, cake stands and ash trays. Some pieces had external decoration in pewter.

Pieces were of good quality, with silky or high leadless glazes, which tended to be thickish in consistency, not always covering the base of pieces.

*Selection of wares. l to r:- i) shallow bowl, 245 mm diam. ii) two-handled vase, 210 mm high iii) lustrous bowl, 231 mm diam. (courtesy of HCMS, DA 1984.114/7; DA 1977.157; CRH 1950.10/42).*

On early wares, a range of ground colours was used, such as black, beige, pink, pale and deep blue, jade and olive green. A characteristic form of decoration was a single band of wavy or zig-zag lines, or instead, a covering of streaky coloured glaze at the top of a piece which was allowed to drip down.

A rare decorative motif was an owl painted centrally on a cake stand, and any recognisable subject other than abstract was rare.

Pieces were mainly produced in monochrome colours, and a favourite colour on later wares appears to have been a bright mottled turquoise-green - a colour which extended across the product range. The turquoise-green wares were often tinged with pink, forming an attractive colour combination.

Later patterned wares were sometimes decorated in an art deco style with simple geometric lines executed in blue, black, brown, red or colour combinations.

The similarity of some early Isle of Wight pieces to some early Poole Pottery pieces is remarkable, and both were known as 'Handcraft Pottery'. Perhaps some of the Poole artists assisted at Carisbrooke.

**References**

*1) Carisbrooke Castle Museum, Newport, Isle of Wight.*

*Selection of wares in 'mottled glaze'.*

| **Type of Ware** | **Production** | **Quality** | **Availability** |
|---|---|---|---|
| Handcraft wares | Moderate | Fair to Good | Uncommon |

**Marks**

| | | | |
|---|---|---|---|
| Incised or printed: | SES | (in monogram within two concentric circles containing the words ISLE OF WIGHT POTTERY CO.) | incised: 1926-c.1933<br>printed: c.1933-1938 |

± letter and number codes.

(On early pieces the numerals indicate the number of the glaze and the letters the shape, in the format numerals/letters. On later wares the first letter indicates the size (M=Medium, S=Small, L=Large), the numbers indicate the shape (up to 229), and the final letter or number the glaze, eg. M/185/4. NB: Early wares bearing the incised mark have unglazed bases; later wares bearing the printed mark have glazed bases.

Some later wares glaze codes: Mottled Glazes: C.4, D.4, 0.4, P.4, Q.4 (4 on its own appears to have been turquoise-green).

Plain Glazes:
E = Natural Semi-Matt
S = Rose Du Barry
A = Green
B = Dark and Light Blue
D = Blue Green
J = Yellow
K = White

# BERNARD LEACH

## St Ives, Cornwall
## artist/potter (1911 - 1979)

### Typical Wares: stonewares, raku, slipware and biscuit, porcelain

### Historical Background

**Bernard Leach erected his pottery at St. Ives in December 1920, with the object of producing a blend of Western and Eastern pottery using his knowledge of Japanese and Oriental pottery styles. He was initially assisted by Shoji Hamada from Kyoto, Japan, and using local materials set about producing hand-crafted pieces, often emulating the Sung and Korai Celadons.**

The Far East was not new to Leach - he had lived there since the age of ten, and by 1920, on his return to England, he had acquired a valuable knowledge of the cultures of China, Korea and Japan. In 1911, whilst in Japan, he had become apprenticed to the Japanese potter Ogata Kenzan, and was able to learn centuries old skills, which set him in good stead for his later work at St Ives.

At St Ives, Leach and Hamada constructed the first traditional Japanese kiln in Western Europe, and two years later the pottery was in full production, producing both high and low temperature stoneware, together with Japanese 'raku' wares (porous fragile stonewares). He employed student apprentices such as Michael Cardew, Katherine Pleydell Bouverie and Norah Braden, who were later to produce pottery in their own right. The early wares, however, were not successful commercially, as they were too dull and monotonous for the British public.

In 1928, after Hamada had returned to Japan, Leach published a pamphlet entitled 'A Potter's Outlook'. This was the forerunner of his famous book 'A Potter's Book', published in 1940, in which he set out standards of description for ceramic pots. His interest in English slipware was spurred on by successful sales in Japan, where it was highly acclaimed, but exhibitions in England could not boost the rather poor sales at home. Pieces were shown at Paterson's Gallery in London, and attracted interest, and from 1930, when Leach's son, David joined the St Ives Pottery, stoneware tiles were produced.

Bernard Leach was a great admirer and friend of Howson Taylor of the Ruskin Pottery and admired generally the work of many English Studio potters, including the Fishley family in the West Country.

In 1934, Bernard Leach returned to Japan for a year's tour of working and lecturing with his Japanese friend Shoji Hamada, the philosopher Soetsu Yanagi, and the potter Tomimoto.

After the war, David Leach took over most of the production management at St Ives, giving his father more time to concentrate on new styles.

Bernard Leach made several further visits to Japan, and exhibited in Northern Europe (1949), the United States (1950, 1958, 1961) New Zealand and Australia (1961), and South America (1966). In 1977, the Victoria and Albert Museum staged a retrospective exhibition of his work, which encouraged dealing in the early pieces in the salerooms.

Bernard Leach died in 1979.

### Products

The early ware at St Ives is very much in the Japanese style, and exhibits an earthy appearance, local unrefined materials having been used for the pottery bodies.

Experiments in slipware gave way to more decorative pieces. The decoration was mostly brush work and sgraffitto, and favourite subjects were birds and leaping fish.

The colours were generally browns and pale greens, and celadon glazes were used, in conjunction with Japanese glazes such as *black* and *kaki iron red*.

Slipware and stoneware were made by Bernard Leach until the late 1930's, after which porcelain and porcellanous stoneware were produced almost exclusively.

Medieval pitchers and pots often influenced the shapes of Leach's pieces in the 1920's, and the Japanese glazes and designs combined to produce a hybrid style.

Vases and bowls were predominant during the 1920's at St Ives, but some

*Shallow dish, 160 mm diam., earthenware with yellow slip decoration on a brown ground, c.1930.*

earthenware dishes were produced mainly about 1929. Models are rare, but some sculptured horses were created during the early 1930's. Tea sets and coffee sets were evident during the mid-1930's at St Ives, and tiles were produced generally from 1930, although some tile panels were produced about 1928.

A yellow galena glaze was frequently used on pieces from the early 1920's, usually on a white slip. Red and dark brown slips were also popular, and colours were generally subdued, and never gaudy.

Pale blue was the brightest colour employed with any regularity, and occasionally light green was used. The designs give more the impression of being executed by colour wash, because of the subdued hues and indefinite outlines.

Landscapes and tree scenes feature strongly on some pieces of the late 1920's and early 1930's, and tree motifs such as 'The Tree of Life' occur throughout the pre-war years.

Some pieces bear mottos, in the English slipware tradition. A globular vase made about 1930, with three handles, bears the motto 'God with us' in sgraffito work, emphasised in dark brown colouring.

Collectors should note that whilst the bulk of Bernard Leach's pots were made at St Ives, some were made on visits abroad at different potteries. From 1911 to 1919, all his pieces (some were only **decorated** by him) were made at potteries in Japan, but all are marked with his monogram.

Prices on the antiques market are high but the quality is good.

**References**

*1) 'The Art of Bernard Leach' (retrospective exhibition catalogue), Victoria & Albert Museum, 1977.*

*2) The Holburne Museum in Bath has a collection of pieces by Bernard Leach, as well as a Crafts Study Centre.*

| **Type of Ware** | **Production** | **Quality** | **Availability** |
|---|---|---|---|
| Art wares | Low to Moderate | Good to Very Good | Uncommon |

**Marks**

| | | |
|---|---|---|
| Painted: | B.H.L. | 1911 - 1913 |
| Trailed Slip: | B.H.L. | 1917 |
| Incised: | BL | 1913 - 1919 |
| Coloured Slip: | BL | 1923 - 1933 |
| Impressed: | BL (in circle) | 1917 - 1919 |
| | BL SI (in circles) | 1921 - 1942 |
| | BL SI | c.1945 |
| | BL (in rectangle) | c 1925 - 1942 |
| | SI (in circle) | |
| | BL SI (block letters in rectangles) | 1943 - c 1946 |

± name of Japanese Pottery

± date

NB: Various permutations of the above marks have been recorded.

# LINTHORPE ART POTTERY

## Middlesbrough (1879-1889)

Typical Wares: art pottery

### Historical Background

**The Linthorpe Art Pottery was established in 1879 by John Harrison in a brickyard known as the 'Sun Brick Works', where deposits of a fine clay could be found.**

The renowned art designer, Christopher Dresser, suggested the setting up of the pottery, which could produce wares to his own designs. Dresser, who had published 'The Art of Decorative Design' in 1862, was one of the first European designers to visit Japan, where, in 1877, he had gathered much useful information about Japanese art and culture, which he later put to good use at the Linthorpe Pottery.

Dresser was retained as Art Director at Linthorpe, and set to work on reproducing Japanese styles, and also primitive South American designs, which though simple in shape, were considered somewhat 'avant-garde' at the time.

The running of the pottery was undertaken by Henry Tooth, an enthusiastic artist and stage designer, who shared Dresser's interest in Japanese art. Dresser was thus left free to concentrate on designs in materials other than ceramics, though it is believed his pottery designs for Linthorpe were considerable in number.

Henry Tooth had no previous pottery-making experience, but by 1883 he had become competent in throwing wares as well as decorating them. From quite early on in the life of the Linthorpe Pottery, Henry Tooth specialised in the use of multi-coloured glazes, and managed to imitate the brilliant colour glazes found on 17th Century and 18th Century Chinese porcelains. He also experimented with streaked and mottled glazes, and produced some striking crackle glaze wares.

In 1882, some Linthorpe pieces were exhibited at the Society of Arts Exhibition in London, and from 1883 to 1885, Linthorpe took its share of prize-winning medals at various world exhibitions.

The short life of the pottery is probably reflected in the fact that Henry Tooth left Linthorpe in 1882 to go into partnership with William Ault and establish the Bretby Art Pottery at Woodville, Derbyshire in 1883. It is noticeable that the pottery designs became less 'avant-garde' after 1882, and that more conventional designs were used. John Harrison, however, was always conscious of the need for pieces to be produced in accordance with the highest principles of art.

A contemporary advertisement speaks of *eastern colouring*, reflecting the oriental influence of Dresser's designs. Certainly, the individual pieces made were of high quality, and although they were inexpensive to buy at the time, their comparative rarity and collectability today demand high prices.

The working conditions at Linthorpe were reported as excellent for the period, and almost 100 people were employed at the pottery. Production only lasted for ten years, however. Competition was strong, and in 1887, prices had to be reduced. The pottery closed in 1889 when John Harrison died, bankrupt.

*Selection of vases designed by Christopher Dresser.*

## Products

In his work, Christopher Dresser imitated South American and Japanese styles, as well as those from the orient. Owing to the varity of glazes available, no two pieces made were exactly alike, and no single style predominated. Pâte-sur-pâte was used as successfully as sgraffito decoration, and on some of the wares a form of impasto decoration was used, where the ornament was placed on the article in the 'biscuit' state.

The items produced at Linthorpe consisted of bottles, plaques, flower-pots, tazzas, salad bowls, fruit bowls, large jardinères, and vases in particular. A range of domestic wares was also introduced, which included cutlery handles (particularly salad servers matching the salad bowls.)

Shapes were generally simple, often bearing characteristic depressions or dimples. Many pieces are similar to Bretby or Ault in style, which is not surprising considering the influence of Henry Tooth at all three potteries.

Painting was much utilised as a form of decoration, and the painted designs executed at Linthorpe included flowers, animals, birds and insects. The colours varied from bright reds to deep blues, and nearly always occurred in monochrome or bichrome combinations, the latter often being a primary colour with a secondary tone, such as red and orange.

Some of the glazes were particularly high, especially those over the streaked designs, sometimes giving the effect of lustre ware. The glazes were also fairly thick, and tended to form a congealed rim on the base of pieces. The quality of the pottery body was low, as is revealed occasionally through unglazed portions on the bases.

The streaked glazes complemented the asymmetrical shapes of Dresser's designs, but after 1882, shapes became simpler and less complicated. Some of Dresser's pieces often incorporated an additional medium such as silver-plated rims and handles.

## Collecting Linthorpe Pottery

Aesthetically there is Linthorpe and Linthorpe. The one is very attractive and decorative, the other mundane and uninteresting. Prices tend to vary according to attraction and quality, though all Linthorpe ware is uncommon, owing to the short life of the pottery. The Dresser designs are the rarest, and will be accordingly priced, but they are also of very good design quality. Any pieces marked with Henry Tooth's monogram are uncommon since he left the pottery in 1882, but such pieces are of mixed quality, and , again, of mixed aesthetic appeal.

**References**


1) *A good selection of Linthorpe may be seen at the Dorman Memorial Museum, Middlesbrough.*

2) *Linthorpe Art Pottery, by C Hart; pub. Aisling Publications, Guisborough, 1988.*

3) *Linthorpe Ware; Exhibition Catalogue (Billingham Art Gallery, Jan. 1970), by J. Le Vine; pub. Teesside Museums & Art Galleries.*

4) *Christopher Dresser 1834 - 1904; Illustrated Catalogue of an Exhibition at the Fine Arts Society, 1972; by Richard Dennis & J Jeffe, pub. Richard Dennis.*

5) *Christopher Dresser 1834 - 1904; Catalogue of an Exhibition held at Camden Arts Centre (1979) and the Dorman Museum, Middlesbrough (1980); by Michael Collins; pub. Arkwright Trust.*

6) *Christopher Dresser, Phd; Catalogue by Andy Tilbrook of an Exhibition by Andy Tilbrook and Dan Klein at the Halkin Arcade, London, Autumn, 1981.*

7) *Linthorpe the Forgotten Pottery; article by Cyril Bracegirdle in Country Life, 1971.*

8) *A Tale of Three Potteries; article by Roger Pinkham in the Antique Collector, September, 1977.*

9) *Christopher Dresser & The Linthorpe Potteries; article by Hilary Wade in The Antique Collector, February, 1984.*


| Type of Ware | Production | Quality | Availability |
|---|---|---|---|
| Art wares signed by Christopher Dresser | Low | Very Good to Excellent | Scarce |
| Other art wares | Low to Moderate | Poor to very Good | Uncommon |

| Marks | | |
|---|---|---|
| Impressed: | LINTHORPE (sometimes with the outline of a vase in the background) | 1879-1889 |
| ± Henry Tooth's monogram impressed: | H T (monogram, large or small) | 1879-1882 |
| ± pattern number up to 4196 | (impressed) | |
| ± Christopher Dresser's mark (up to pattern number 1700), in impressed signature, sometimes incised or painted. | Chr. Dresser | 1879-1882 |
| ± artist's mark: | e.g. William Metcalf, Arthur Shorter, Rachel Smith, Clara Pringle, Lucy Worth, Florence Minto, Thomas Hudson, Arthur Fuller, William Davidson, Fred Brown. | |

# THE MARTIN BROTHERS (artist/potters)

## Southall, Middlesex (1873-1915)

Typical Wares: saltglaze stoneware

### Historical Background

**Also in the category of artist/potters were the four Martin brothers (Robert Wallace, Walter, Edwin and Charles), who produced salt-glaze stoneware based on Doulton techniques, but using their own designs.**

They commenced production in 1873 at the Fulham Pottery, but moved to Southall in 1877. Charles Martin kept a shop and gallery in High Holborn, which acted as the retail outlet for the pottery. Wallace Martin was deemed head of the firm, and was concerned mainly with modelling the wares. Walter Martin was the principal thrower, whilst Edwin Martin's role was as principal decorator. Both Walter and Edwin had previously worked as assistants in Doulton's Art Studios, and had attended evening classes at Lambeth School of Art from 1872 to 1873. The brothers often interchanged roles but also relied on outside help. The celebrated Mark V Marshall assisted at one time as a decorator before moving on to Doulton, and an artist by the name of W E Willey was also employed.

During the late 1890's the Martin Brothers came under the patronage of the archtitect Sydney Greenslade. The *vegetable* designs of this time resulted through one of his commissions to the brothers. He proved influential to the brothers' business, persuading them to accompany him to the Paris Exhibition of 1900, where they collected many new ideas.

After 1900, however, business began to fall steadily, resulting in the closure of the pottery in 1914, the shop closing not long afterwards.

### Products

The early pieces are much sought after by collectors, and consist of carved and modelled medieval-like wares. Apart from some early terra-cotta ware, production was exclusively salt-glaze stoneware. The pieces were often carved and incised, and possessed a Gothic appearance.

Vases and pots were mainly produced, but about 1883, sculptured models of birds and animals were introduced. Many of the birds had detachable heads for use as tobacco jars, and some of the birds and animals were grotesque in shape, often resulting from errors in throwing the clay. The practice of using rejects for modelling into grotesques not only reduced waste, but was also profitable, since the grotesques were in popular demand. The Brannam Pottery were later to adopt a similar practice.

The contemporary writer, Cosmo Monkhouse, wrote in 1882 of the Martin Brothers' grotesques: 'A strangely human jug completes a group of creatures like many things, and yet like nothing on earth'. Concerning the brothers' vases, he wrote: 'there is scarcely any variety of decoration which is not employed'. Certainly some of the vases are extremely beautiful. There was a high degree of modelling on all pieces, and the patterns used were emphasised by colours such as cobalt blue, and later on, shades of brown. All shapes and sizes exist, from finely detailed miniatures to pieces of substantial size. Many vases lean at unusual angles and some are square in shape.

Apart from the humanesque features of the animal and bird models, there were dragon motifs and fish designs created during the 1880's and 1890's. The late 1890's saw the creation of textured vases

*Stoneware examples. l to r:- i) 'Wally bird' jar and cover, 200 mm high, marked 'R.W.Martin & Brothers London & Southall 10-4- 1903'. ii) vase, 306 mm high, incised decoration of sea creatures, marked 'R.W.Martin & Brothers 8-1891 London & Southall'.*

and pots resembling vegetables. These are now comparatively rare as are the well known 'face jugs' (jugs modelled with grinning faces), which were made about the same period. The vegetable pots exhibit fine texturing and modelling, and were made in a wide variety of shapes.

Floral motifs are also to be found, with a favourite subject being the foxglove. Art nouveau swirls of stylised leaves were also a popular form of decoration, heavily incised of course, with a single colour glaze covering.

Other wares consisted of fountains and large garden ornaments, cornices, mantlepieces, plaques and bas-reliefs, miniatures, figurines, jars, clock- cases, and even chess-men and oil-lamp bodies. Many items were sold privately, and were costly in comparison with other studio pottery of the time. Ten guineas was not an unusual price to pay for a Martin Brothers vase of say only eight inches high.

## Collecting Martin Brothers Pottery

The Martin Brothers' stoneware is highly valued by collectors, not only for its rarity, but also for its simplicity of design and individual style. To some, the ware is dull and lacking in colour, but one must remember that the Brothers were firstly modellers and throwers, and only secondly decorators. One cannot compare the decoration of their wares with the brilliance of De Morgan's pieces, for example. We are talking about skilled sculptors of clay on the one hand and a great ceramic chemist and decorator on the other. One just has to see the expressions on the Brothers' face-jugs and grotesques to realise the skill of their work in clay modelling.

The decoration was secondary, but it is nonetheless good. Some of the bamboo-like vases are truly representative of bamboo wood, and all the texture of this material is deftly reproduced in clay by skillful sgraffito work.

The early 'medieval' vases are intricately worked, and one is often allowed to appreciate the natural beauty of the stoneware body sometimes left uncoloured below the mellow saltglaze covering.

Collectors should be aware that some pottery marked 'Martinware' was made until the 1930's by Wallace Martin's son, Clement Martin; but this is of poorer quality than the earlier ware.

**References**

*1) Southall Library houses many fine examples of the Martin Brothers' work.*

*2) The Victoria & Albert Museum, London.*

*3) The Heritage Museum, Kingston-upon-Thames has a small collection of fine pieces, the result of a local bequest.*

*4) Pitshanger Manor Museum, Walpole Park, Ealing, West London.*

*5 'The Martin Brothers, Potters' by Malcolm Haslam; pub. Richard Dennis, 1978.*

*6 'The Martin Brothers' by Angela Summerfield; article in The Antique Collector magazine, November, 1987.*

| **Type of Ware** | **Production** | **Quality** | **Availability** |
|---|---|---|---|
| Saltglaze stoneware: modelled birds/ animals/face jugs/ grotesques | Low | Good to Very Good | Scarce |
| vases | Low to Medium | Poor to Very Good | Uncommon |
| plaques | Low | Poor to Very Good | Scarce |

**Marks**

| | | | |
|---|---|---|---|
| Impressed: (with variations) | R W MARTIN<br>FULHAM | | (1873/4) |
| | R W MARTIN fecit | | (1874/7) |
| | R W MARTIN<br>LONDON | | (1874/7) |
| | R W MARTIN<br>SOUTHALL | | (1877/8) |
| Signed, incised in clay before firing | R W Martin Sc<br>Southall | R W Martin Sc<br>London | (1877/8) |
| | R W Martin<br>London & Southall<br>7-1889* | | (1879/c.1883) |
| | R W Martin & Brothers<br>London & Southall | | (1883/1914) |
| | Martin Bros.<br>London 4-1906* | | (1883/1914) |

± artist's initials and thrower's initials
RWM - Robert Wallace Martin
WFM - Walter Frazer Martin
EBM - Edwin Bruce Martin

± date (month and year of manufacture)*

# MAW & CO.

## Benthall Works, Broseley, Shropshire. (1850-1967)

Typical Wares: tiles, earthenware, lustres, pâte-sur-pâte

### Historical Background

**Originally established by George and Arthur Maw at Worcester in 1850, Maw & Co. transferred their encaustic tile making business to Ironbridge Gorge at Benthall, Shropshire in 1852.**

From 1851, mostly plain tiles with geometric patterns were produced, but from 1857 new colours were introduced enabling greater pattern flexibility. In 1861, the firm began to produce small tesserae for use in pictorial mosaics, either as wall or floor decoration. Not long after, coloured enamels were produced for majolica tiles, and in 1867, Maw & Co. exhibited their renowned turquoise blue enamel at an exhibition in Paris.

In 1882, a new enlarged 'Benthall Works' was established at nearby Jackfield, but tiles remained the principal output of the firm, the production of which was facilitated by clay pits adjacent to the factory.

From the late 1880's, the production of art pottery increased, and work was commissioned from well-known artists both in this area and in the design of tiles. The artists Lewis Day and Walter Crane contributed significantly to Maw & Co.'s output, and tiles by them were exhibited at the Royal Jubilee Exhibition at Manchester in 1887.

Maw & Co. won many medals at international exhibitions, including Dublin, Paris, Oporto and Melbourne (1888- 9). They also exhibited at Glasgow in 1888 and at the Chicago World's Fair in 1893, the trade-stand of which was designed by Charles Henry Temple, their chief designer. His monogram appears on several wares from about 1885 to 1901.

Maw & Co. established a world-wide reputation for their decorations, and undertook several commissions for decorative work, including the Maharaja's Palace at Mysore in India.

The company ceased trading as Maw & Co. in 1967, and the Benthall Works at Jackfield is now a crafts centre.

### Products

During the late 1870's, Maw & Co. produced a range of lustre decorated wares similar to those of William De Morgan, and like De Morgan's pieces, a common decorative subject was the galleon. Lustre glazes were used to good effect on vases, jugs and tazzas, but sgraffito decoration and pâte-sur-pâte were also employed as decorative methods.

Charles Henry Temple's favourite decorative subject seems to have been the draped classical female figure, but he also produced wares with relief-moulded floreate patterns, some of which were on a green ground with brown lustre glaze.

Favourite decorative themes of Walter Crane were Grecian ships or naked female figures in floreate motifs. Crane often used a simple gold or ruby lustre on a white ground for his decorations. From 1885, he designed some vases, ewers and plates in a Mediterranean style, reminiscent of

*Vases designed by Walter Crane. (courtesy Clive House Museum, Shrewsbury) Photo by G T Prince*

Italian Renaissance pottery. These also incorporated his favourite forms of decoration, often in monochrome lustres on a white ground, but with some accompanying relief moulding, such as swan's head handles to vases or ewers. These wares were produced until about 1915. A catalogue of 'Maw's Decorative Pottery' for 1900 lists a variety of ornamental wares and decoration, as shown below.

Objects for decoration ranged from large urns and jardinères to chargers and vases, many featuring heavy use of modelling. A series of moulded plates and chargers was advertised as 'subjects adapted from designs of fine antique silver'. These subjects included 17 personalities from 1491 to 1653, such as Henry VII, Mary Queen of Scots, Lord Darnly, Shakespeare and Cromwell. Many of the other objects imitated classical or antique pottery styles from the Mediterranean.

Tiles, however, were the principal output of the Company, and with the increase in colours and the introduction of enamel colours they became an attractive medium for the attention of competent artists. Walter Crane designed a nursery-rhyme series for tiles about 1874, featuring characters such as 'Little Boy Blue' and 'Little Brown Betty'. They were similar to his illustrations with music for 'The Baby's Opera' (1877).

About 1890, Maw & Co. produced a range of dust- pressed, hand- painted ruby lustre tiles in art nouveau floreate designs. The *dust-pressed* technique was a quick and easy method of producing tiles from dry 'dust' clay using machinery. Maw & Co. also employed the 'plastic clay' method, where clay of one colour was pressed into clay of another, and smoothed down. The 'encaustic sandwich' method was also used for floor tiles, where strips or blocks of clay of different colours were inlaid. A further process involved 'tubelining' the outline of a decoration to give an effect of relief.

The dust-pressed technique could also produce 'mosaic effect' tiles; and the collector will come across trade tiles which advertise the many finishes and sizes available from Maw & Co.

From 1905 to around 1915, colourful embossed tiles were produced, often featuring the galleon theme; and about the same time Lewis Day designed many embossed tiles with richly decorated floral motifs.

During the 1930's, many tiles in the art deco style were produced (small four inch tiles in particular). These had strong geometric patterns with low relief 'eggshell' glazes which exhibited a metallic sheen.

**References**

*1) Clive House Museum, Shrewsbury. (tiles)*
*2) Kensington Palace Gardens, Kensington, London (c.1862)*
*3) Jackfield Tile Collection, Ironbridge Gorge Museum, Jackfield.*
*4) Arthur Maw's house, now the Valley Hotel, Ironbridge. 5) Watts Gallery, Compton, Surrey. (some vases)*

**Artist's Marks**

Walter Crane (died 1915)
'CW' + crane bird in monogram

Lewis F Day 'LFD' in monogram

C H Temple 'CHT' (c 1885-1901)

*Ornamental wares and decoration from "Maw's Decorative Pottery" Catalogue (1900)*

| | |
|---|---|
| 1) Rich Persian Glazes | : 'beautiful colours' on modelled surfaces; 'marbled' or 'splashed' colours, intermixed or layered 'after the manner of the Oriental potters'. These glazes were available across the object range. |
| 2) Polychrome Enamel Decoration | : combined with painting on modelled features, 'after Palissy or Della Robbia'. Mostly on urns and heavily moulded items. |
| 3) Under-glaze Painting | : on plain surfaces, sometimes accompanied by enamel painting or gilding. |
| 4) Barbotine, or Clay Painting | : 'impasto' painting on vases in a floreate Persian style. |
| 5) Incised Ware | : intricate sgraffito work on vases, covered with transparent glazes. |
| 6) Oiron, or Henri Deux Ware | : as for Incised Ware but 'the indentation is filled in with coloured clays and the whole is covered with a transparent colourless glaze'. |
| 7) Sgraffito | : decoration incised through a layer of different coloured clay producing a cameo effect. |
| 8) Lustre Ware | : available across the product range. |

| Type of Ware | Production | Quality | Availability |
|---|---|---|---|
| Tiles | High | Fair to Good | Abundant |
| Lustre wares (signed) | Low | Good to Very Good | Scarce |
| Art Pottery | Low | Good | Scarce |

**Marks**

| | | |
|---|---|---|
| Impressed: | FLOREAT MAW SALOPIA (in circle) | c.1880 |
| ± BROSELEY SALOP (on tiles) | | |
| ± the words 'DOUBLE' AND 'GRIP' enclosed in separate circles, on tiles. | | |
| Painted and later moulded: | MAW & CO | c 1885-1915 |
| ± artist's mark | MAW | c 1850 onwards |

# MINTONS (1793 to present)

## South Kensington Art Pottery Studio (1871-1875) & Stoke-on-Trent

### Typical Wares: art wares 1871 to present, pâte sur pâte, majolica ware, earthenware, tiles, 'reduced' glazes from 1914

### Historical Background

**Mintons began in 1793, when Thomas Minton set up the first works. From 1845 to 1872, the firm was known as Minton & Co., whilst from 1873 to the present time it was known as Mintons Ltd.**

The establishment of an Art Pottery in South Kensington, London, was prompted by the success of the artist E J Poynter, who was responsible for the decoration of the tiled grill-room of the South Kensington Museum (now the Victoria & Albert Museum). In 1871, a Studio was set up near the Royal College of Music, under the art directorship of W S Coleman. Here tiles were produced with several plaques by Coleman himself, which sold from thirty pounds upwards.

Hannah Barlow was a decorator at the Studio, previous to her joining Doulton, and there were several competent artists engaged in work during the Studio's lifetime, notably John Eyre (a member of the Royal Society of British Artists) and E Reuter (connected with Mintons from 1874 to 1895). The Studio was never a successful venture and was not re-opened when fire broke out in 1875, W S Coleman having left two years previously.

The closure of the South Kensington Studio did not end the production of art pottery at Mintons. On the contrary, Mintons saw the rest of the century out with many fine pottery creations, thanks to the skill and enterprise of its art directors and artists themselves. The art directors are worth listing here, since each contributed some special talent to the pottery:-

From 1845, M Hollins, a partner in the Company, undertook the production of tiles through the subsidiary firm of Minton, Hollins & Co. Although some tiles were produced under the title 'Minton & Co', the majority were produced and marked by Hollins' subsidiary Company.

Mintons were perhaps more renowned for their tile products during the mid-Victorian period than for the superb dinner services which they currently produce.

In 1902, Léon V Solon and John Wadsworth introduced a new ware based on Viennese art nouveau designs, which became known as Secessionist Ware. The striking use of colour combinations (such as crimson against green) and the stylised nouveau floral patterns ensured the success of this ware for several years.

Today the name 'Mintons' continues as a trade-mark of Royal Doulton Limited, but the individual style of their tablewares has been assured.

### Products

Although tiles were produced in quantity by Minton Hollins & Co., they were also part of the output of the South Kensington Studio.

During the early part of 1871, W S Coleman produced an initial series of tiles and other items decorated by means of underglaze painting, but later on, tube-line decoration became a favoured method on tiles.

Tube-line decoration consisted of creating raised lines of trailed slip using a tubular tool, and, with the application of coloured glazes, it gave an added dimension to tiles or vases.

Some fine tile designs were carried out by the artist E J Poynter and Walter Crane during the Kensington Studio period.

Under the direction of Léon Arnoux (1849-1895), a range of so- called 'majolica ware' was produced, decorated in relief by Arnoux's 'majolica' glazes. The items produced in this range (fountains, jardinères and other garden ornaments) bore little relation to actual majolica ware, except by appearance. The range proved popular, however, and sold well into the turn of the century.

From 1870, printed and painted dinner services were produced at Mintons, and the more important pieces were signed, by such painters as H W Foster (figures) and J E Dean (animals).

From 1901 to 1909, Léon V Solon was art director at Mintons. Solon pioneered the pâte-sur-pâte process, and himself produced some spectacular bottles and vases using this method. Some splendid examples of these, in white on blue, can be seen at the Victoria & Albert Museum, London.

The pâte-sur-pâte process (literally 'paste on paste') involved building up layers of white clay slips - a technique developed by Solon whilst at the Sevres factory in France. The decoration was then cut into the piece before firing.

Solon's styles were mainly classical and from the time that he joined Mintons (1870), the company was greatly influenced by the rich colourings if items produced by the Sevres porcelain factory. So much so, that Mintons employed continental artists in an attempt to

| | |
|---|---|
| Léon Arnoux | French Chemist and potter, art director 1849-95 |
| Louis Jahn | (1895 - 1900) |
| Léon V Solon | (1901 - 1909) |
| John William Wadsworth | (1909 - 1914) |
| Walter Woodman | (1914 - 1930) |
| Reginald Haggar | (1930 - 1935) |
| John William Wadsworth | (1935 - 1955) |

emulate some of the Sevres styles. Pâte-sur-pâte was successful at Mintons, and was revived by A. Birks as a means of decoration in the 1920's.

The production of earthenware art nouveau vases was also undertaken at Mintons during Solon's directorship. The most noticeable range was the Secessionist Ware, which appeared on many vase forms as well as jardinères, candlesticks, etc.

After 1909, during J W Wadsworth's direction, many fine art- nouveau floral motifs were executed on vases, cups and saucers, and dessert plates.

During the Edwardian era some Mintons pieces were cast from models by French sculptors but generally pieces were hand-thrown. A common colour combination of this period was green, yellow and pastel blue, which appeared across a wide range of articles.

Tiles were still being produced in quantity with some 10" and 4" tiles in limited production. The artist G E Cook executed some fine monochrome portraits on 4" tiles.

During the 1914-18 war, Minton Hollins & Co produced an ornamental ware under the title 'Astra Ware'. The ware originated through the slump in the tile trade as a result of the war, and proved so successful that production continued after 1918. It sold at a moderate price, and consisted of items with variegated decoration in the glaze, created by reduction in the kiln. The variegations ranged from bright reds to sea-greens, with bubbles of coloured glaze in relief. The texture varied considerably as did the shapes and sizes of the pieces, which ranged from small buttons and medallions to bowls and vases.

During the early 1920's, the craze for floating-flower bowls was admirably satisfied by Mintons, who produced a wide range of pieces for this purpose.

A general characteristic of Minton's ware is the richness and brightness of colour used. Under the direction of Reginald Haggar (from 1930) more modern designs began to appear which were widely reflected in the ranges of tableware. Stylised landscapes were depicted in the 'Landscape' pattern, but the more typical deco geometric patterns were also produced.

Under John Wadsworth's second period of direction, new ranges of earthenware were launched, such as 'Solano Ware' (from 1937) and a bright deco pattern called 'Byzantine' (1938).

## Collecting Mintons Pottery

The most widely collected Mintons pieces are those produced under the Studio conditions. The selection available is large, and the quality variable. Paired items are often evident, whether vases or candlesticks, and styles were very much dependent on the vogue or fashion of the time.

Minton tiles of the Victorian period are popular with collectors, and are widely available at the time of writing. Their relatively low price and good quality enables them to be put to original use.

| **Type of Ware** | **Production** | **Quality** | **Availability** |
|---|---|---|---|
| Tiles | High to Very High | Fair to Good (signed tiles often Very Good) | Abundant |
| Pâte-sur-pâte (early) | Low | Very Good to Excellent | Scarce |
| Earthenware | Moderate to High | Good to Very Good | Abundant |

**Marks**

| | | | |
|---|---|---|---|
| Printed: | MINTON'S Art Pottery STUDIO Kensington Gore | (in circle) | 1871-1875 |
| Impressed: | MINTONS ENGLAND | | 1890-1910 |
| Printed: | MINTON LTD | | 1900-1908 |
| | Mintons No. 1 | | c.1910 |
| Impressed or printed: | MINTON HOLLINS & CO | | 1928 |
| Printed | (Globe surmounted by a crown with legend: "Mintons England") | | 1873-1912 |
| | (as above but with laurel leaves and legend: "Mintons Est 1793") | | 1912-1950 |

± Artist's Mark

± Year mark (1842 - 1942)


**References**

1) *Dictionary of Minton, by Paul Atterbury; pub. Antique Collectors' Club, 1988.*

2) *'Minton 1798-1910'; catalogue of an Exhibition by E. Aslin & Paul Atterbury at the Victoria & Albert Museum, London, 1976; pub. V & A.*

3) *'Minton Tiles 1835-1935'; catalogue of an Exhibition, edited by D. Skinner & Hans van Lemmen; pub. Stoke-on-Trent City Museum & Art Gallery, 1984.*

4) *'Minton Secessionist Ware'; article by Grant Mutler in the Connoisseur, Aug., 1980.*

# WILLIAM MOORCROFT artist/potter (b.1872; d.1945)

## MacIntyre & Co. (1898-1913) Cobridge (1913-1945)

Typical Wares: earthenware, flambé, lustres

**William Moorcroft was born at Burslem, the son of a gifted artist. He was educated at the Wedgwood Institute, Burslem, and later at South Kensington, where he came under the influence of the styles of William Morris and of the artist Walter Crane. In 1897, he gained his Art Master's Certificate, but instead of starting work as a teacher, he took up a job as designer with the established pottery of James MacIntyre & Co.**

### 1) At James MacIntyre & Co, Washington Works, Burslem (1898 - 1913)

#### Historical Background

From 1898, William Moorcroft was in charge of the art pottery department at James MacIntyre & Co. He formed a group of decorators, decorating art pieces, many of which were marketed by Liberty of London.

At MacIntyre he was responsible not only for the decoration of the ware, but also for its production. In 1904, he was awarded the gold medal for pottery at the St Louis Exhibition - the first of many awards throughout his lifetime.

In 1913, MacIntyre's art pottery department closed, and Moorcroft set up his own business at Cobridge.

#### Products

At MacIntyre Moorcroft drew all his own designs, which were 'slip-trailed' on to the pots, using a tubular tool.

The main ware produced was entitled *Florian Ware* which consisted of art nouveau floral designs of cornflowers, poppies, violets etc.

The colours were derived from metallic oxides, and were applied under the glaze, except on some gilded pieces - gilding being used only for a short period before being abandoned. The ware was fired at least twice at very high temperatures.

From 1902, Moorcroft evolved a landscape pattern with mushroom headed trees which was called *Hazledene*, whilst the following year saw the development of a style of fungi in raised outline which he called *Claremont*.

The familiar *Pomegranite* theme was not introduced until 1911, and generally all the floral themes, whether natural or abstract, were executed against a white or cream background, the outlines being generally blue or green in colour.

From 1905, Moorcroft produced some red and green lustre wares, which he termed *Flamminian Ware*, and a gold coloured ware entitled *Aurelian Ware*.

In his designs, Moorcroft was strongly influenced by Persian and Turkish decoration, and in his potting, the simple shapes of the 5th Century Grecian vessels attracted him.

He was able to combine the two styles admirably on a range of products which consisted of such items as flower-pots, flower vases, tobacco jars, jugs and biscuit barrels. Some of these pieces (such as biscuit barrels and tobacco jars) were mounted in silver, whilst other pieces (such as tazzas and some vases) were mounted in 'TUDRIC' Pewter', and so marked.

Tudric Pewter was a brand name of Liberty (1903 to 1938). It was Celtic inspired in design and the pewter had a high silver content.

Liberty also marketed "Florian Ware" which proved so popular that market outlets were also established by MacIntyre at Tiffany of New York and Rouard of Paris.

### 2) At Cobridge. (W Moorcroft Limited) 1913 - 1945

#### Historical Background

Having founded his own firm at Cobridge, Moorcroft continued to produce his own individual brand of pottery. He took on some of the redundant potters and decorators from MacIntyre as assistants, and worked alongside them until 1937, when he was joined by his son Walter Moorcroft.

From 1919, Moorcroft began to develop his famous flambé glazes, using a specially built kiln. He pioneered the search for a wider range of underglaze colours that would withstand the high temperatures of the kiln, and his knowledge as a chemist proved invaluable in this task. To Moorcroft, his flambé ware was his finest achievement, and it was widely acclaimed throughout the world.

Pieces were exhibited annually at the British Industies Fair, Olympia, London from 1915 to 1939, and Queen Mary made a purchase from the Moorcroft Stand at the British Industrial Arts Exhibition, 1920. The Queen collected Moorcroft pieces for some years, and in 1928, William Moorcroft received the Royal Warrant as 'Potter to Her Majesty the Queen'. This

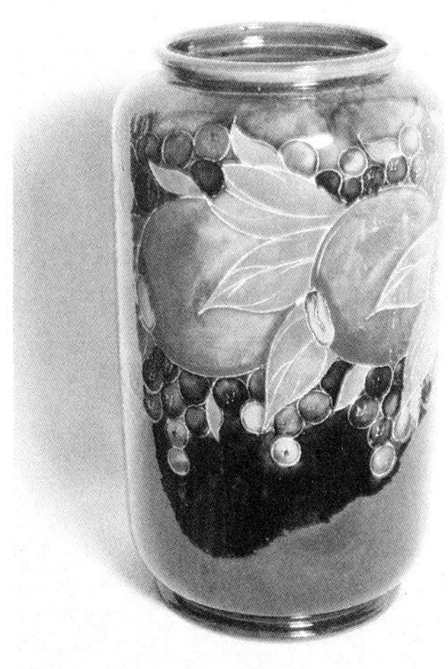

*Vase, 270 mm high, pomegranites and berries.*

title appears as part of the mark on all his wares made since then until 1945.

During the 1930's the demand for decorated studio pottery dwindled on the home market, but in spite of the fact that many of the well known pottery art departments were closing down, Moorcroft continued to produce decorated wares, and evolve new techniques and designs. The continental market was still healthy, however, and Moorcroft was careful to keep alive his contacts abroad. Consequently, there was more pottery exported during this time than was produced for the home market.

During the Second World War, when even the continental market had disappeared, Moorcroft just managed to keep the business going ready for his son to return from the war and enter the firm.

In 1945, William Moorcroft died, aged

| Type of Ware | Production | Quality | Availabilty |
|---|---|---|---|
| Florian Ware (at MacIntyre) and other named wares 1898 - 1913 | Low to Moderate | Good to Very Good | Uncommon to Scarce |
| Non-domestic art wares, 1913 - 1945 | Moderate to High | Good to Excellent | Common |
| Blue domestic ware | High | Fair to Good | Common |
| Flambé wares 1919-1945 | Moderate | Good to Excellent | Uncommon |

**Marks**

| | | |
|---|---|---|
| Printed: | James MacIntyre * & Co Buslem (in brown in circular motif) (+ Moorcroft's painted signature in green) | 1898-1913 |
| Transfer Printed: | FLORIAN WARE (in brown in motif) (+ Moorcroft's painted signature in green) | 1898-1904 |

* this mark, with variations, occurs on pottery made at MacIntyre's from 1860 to 1930 without Moorcroft's signature. Only those pieces in which Moorcroft had a hand were marked with his signature.

| | | |
|---|---|---|
| Printed underglaze: | W Moorcroft (signed in green until early 1920's thence in blue, except on flambé wares) | 1913-1945 |
| | WM (signed in blue) | (on smaller articles) |
| ± 'W Moorcroft Potter to HM the Queen' | stamped on base (1928 - 1945) | |
| ± year painted on base | (rare) | 1913-1945 |
| ± removable paper label * 'By Appointment W Moorcroft Potter to HM The Queen' | | (1930 - 1945) |
| ± stamped or incised lettering and numbers | | 1913 - 1945 |
| ± 'MOORCROFT' or 'MOORCROFT BURSLEM' | stamped | 1913 - 1921 (+ 'ENGLAND' c1916 - 1921) |
| ± 'MOORCROFT MADE IN ENGLAND' | stamped | 1921 - 1930 |

* Walter Moorcroft Pottery has a similar but different label.

(NB: It is not yet established as to what the 'O' or 'X' marks mean that occur on some pieces).

73. His son Walter took over the Cobridge works, and continued making Moorcroft pottery until 1986. The business continues today, having been saved from liquidation, and new wares are planned.

## Products

Pieces made from 1913 show an improvement in the quality of the pottery body. The floral designs were continued, and adapted to each new colour or glaze that Moorcroft invented.

Fish designs were popular, as were trees in landscapes and many types of fruit and flower motifs, particularly the pansy, and pomegranite with berries. Most early decorations were executed on a white ground, but Moorcroft made widespread use of a pale celadon green background which contrasted well with the rich colours of many of his subjects. With the development of richer colours of decoration, a deep blue was often employed as the background colour. During the 1930's, however, there was a general trend towards paler colours.

In 1913, Moorcroft produced a popular range of 'powder blue' tableware for domestic use. Although each piece was hand thrown, production was high, continuing for fifty years.

From 1919, flambé decorated pieces were produced of exceptional quality. These were mostly vases or plates of simple shape, but often massed with colour. The early flambé wares were dark in tone, in contrast to the later pieces which were brighter, the outlines being more distinct. On many flambé pieces, the flambé glaze overlaps on to the undecorated base giving a red sprayed appearance. No two pieces of flambé ware were made exactly alike.

Besides the decorative flambé ware, Moorcroft also produced some lustre ware in monochrome, and some monochrome vases (in celadon or blue). The lustre glazes were applied over printed motifs, and occured in bright colours such as reds, greens, blues and yellows, etc. They were not so successful commercially and were discontinued in the early 1920's.

During the early 1930's, some fine plain flambé dinner plates were produced in stoneware. Also, during the 1930's, an interesting pattern of waving corn in pale colour on pale pastel backgrounds was produced.

## Collecting Moorcroft Pottery

William Moorcroft's pottery was virtually unknown in the antiques trade fifteen years ago, but a surge of interest grew up after the 1973 exhibition of his work at the Victoria and Albert Museum, London. It is now extremely popular amongst collectors, commanding high prices in spite of the high output.

The fact that each piece is an art piece of high quality, and that each is signed as such, enhances the high reputation that this pottery has on the antiques market. The earlier wares are fairly scarce and exhibit a style which is similar but different from the later wares.

Walter Moorcroft wares are similar in design to many of those made prior to 1945, but the colours are brighter. The collector should be extremely wary in differentiating pieces. There is much Walter Moorcroft sold as being of the c. 1936 - 45 period, often quite unintentionally.

The collector should be aware of Moorcroft imitations which were produced during the 1920's, such as Royal Stanley's *Jacobean Ware* (mostly berries and leaves in dark colours) and Hancock & Co's *Morris Ware* (imitating Moorcroft's MacIntyre Florian style). These wares are well recognised, however, and much collected in their own right.

**References**

*1) Moorcroft Pottery, by Paul Atterbury; pub. Richard Dennis & H Edwards, 1987*

*2) 'William Moorcroft and Walter Moorcroft (1897-1973)'; catalogue of an exhibition at the Fine Arts Society, 1973; pub. Richard Dennis.*

*3) 'The Art Pottery of Mr William Moorcroft'; article by Fred Miller in The Art Jounal, 1903.*

*4) 'William Moorcroft - A Critical Appreciation'; article by John Bemrose in Pottery & Glass, June, 1943.*

*A selection of wares made at Cobridge (post 1913).*

# BERNARD MOORE artist/chemist

## Longton, Staffs. (1870-1905)
## Wolfe Street, Stoke-on- Trent (1905-1915)

### Typical Wares: earthenwares, porcelain, flambé, crystalline & other glaze effects

### Historical Background

**Bernard Moore was born in 1850, the elder son of a Staffordshire potter named Samuel Moore.**

In 1870, Bernard, together with his brother Samuel Vincent Moore, took over the running of their father's china works at Longton, becoming known as Moore Brothers. Bernard also worked as a consultant in bone china for several pottery firms, but it was not until many years later that he set up his own studio in Stoke-on-Trent.

At Moore Brothers, richly coloured Victorian china and porcelain were produced, and styles frequently imitated those of the Orient, with a high degree of modelling.

The company exhibited widely, winning a gold medal at the Sydney Interanational Exhibition in 1879, the Melbourne International Exhibition in 1881 and the World's Columbian Exhibition at Chicago in 1893.

From 1901, Bernard Moore began to experiment with flambé glazes and other reducing glaze effects, using imported Chinese blanks. His experiments were conducted on a part-time basis in collaboration with Cuthbert Bailey at Doulton & Co., thus giving him access to Doulton's modern laboratory. The experiments were successful, and both Moore and Doulton were acclaimed as having rediscovered the secret of the ancient Chinese flambe glazes.

These early pieces were certainly influenced by Oriental styles and shapes, and reflected the popular interest at the time in ancient Oriental styles, the Chinese Sung period in particular.

Moore's brother Samuel died in 1890, and by 1905 Bernard had sold the china business in order to set up his own studio. In setting up his studio in 1905 in Wolfe Street, Stoke- on-Trent, he engaged many local art school graduates as well as pupils from the Royal College of Art. The studio was solely a decorating establishment, however, all the pottery bodies being brought in from elsewhere, in particular Mintons and Wedgwood.

Bernard Moore produced many fine examples of his distinctive rouge flambe glazed pottery at his studio, exhibiting pieces at international exhibitions, but some of his best pieces were lost at the Brussels International Exhibition of 1910 when the British Industrial Hall housing the exhibits was totally destroyed by fire. Moore also exhibited at the Turin International Exhibition of 1911.

Moore's highly individual creations were costly to produce, and even more expensive to purchase. They were, however, popular with the Royal family and upper classes, and Queen Mary (who frequently patronised Moorcroft's wares) was known to have purchased pieces at the British Industrial Arts Exhibition as well as visiting Moore's showroom on her tour of the Staffordshire Potteries in 1913.

It seems that production at the studio ceased in 1915, although Bernard Moore exhibited pieces at the British Industrial Arts Exhibition in 1920. Whether anything had been produced since 1915 is not clear, although some pieces in existence show a Minton date code for 1920.

In later life, Moore concentrated on the science of ceramic production, publishing several papers in technical journals and

*Selection of flambe wares. l to r:- i) vase, 145 mm high, with enamelled decoration of stylised dragons. ii) tall vase, 210 mm high, flambe glaze, by Evelyn Hope Beardmore. iii) miniature vase, 50 mm high, with enamelled decoration of stylised dragons. iv) vase, 175 mm high, with enamelled Chinese inspired decoration.*

acting as adviser to many pottery firms. He died in 1935, aged 84.

## Products

With the exception of some experimental wares (1901-1905), pieces produced at the china works of Moore Brothers differ completely from those produced at Moore's Studio.

At the studio both plain and decorative flambé pieces were produced, most having a high glaze. Favourite subjects were ships, Oriental dragons, fish, fruit and floral motifs; but the collector will come across many other subjects, particularly animals and birds, such as owls and ducks, and combinations of subjects such as flying bats with stars.

Among the artists employed by Moore at the studio were Evelyn Hope Beardmore, Hilda Carter, Dora Billington, Reginald Robert Tomlinson, Annie Ollier, Hilda Lindop, Edward R Wilkes, Cicely H Jackson and John Adams (later to become director of the Poole Potteries).

In all, eight 'glaze effects' are listed in a Moore's publicity booklet: *Peach Blow* (resembling the skin of a peach fruit, pink and pale green), *Haricot, Rouge Flambe, Lustre, Sang-de-boeuf* (produced by using copper oxides fused in a reducing kiln), *Gold Flambé* (produced by dissolving liquid gold chloride and fusing in a reducing kiln), *Hispano-Moresque* and *Transmutation Glazes.*

Some crystalline glazes were also produced, as well as *Persian blues* and *aventurine* glazes. Pate- sur-pate was successfully used as a means of decoration (mainly on pilgrim bottles) and was often accompanied by lavish gilding.

Several small pieces were also used for flambé decoration, such as miniature vases and bowls. Shapes generally were simple, ranging from deep bowls to shallow plates, and relying on the beauty of the glaze for effect.

Because all the pieces for decorating were bought in, a mixture of pottery bodies was used, from thinly potted porcellanous wares to thickly potted earthenwares.

Modelled figures were also decorated, mainly of small animals, fish and birds, such as frogs, ducks, cats, rabbits, mice and monkeys. These are fairly scarce (although a considerable number were fired); and many incorporate Oriental motifs. The origin of the models, however, is not clear, but many were known to be imported from Europe.

Bernard Moore is perhaps better remembered for his rouge flambé vases and ginger- jars, which in the full panoply of their densely streaked glazes are without parallel. Unfortunately, many of the finest pieces are in the possession of Moore's heirs and descendants and so are not readily available for viewing.

## Collecting Bernard Moore Pottery

The short life of the Studio and the relatively low production of Moore's work, together with its individuality, have made it popular with collectors. The flambé pieces are of good quality, but easily subject to scratching. Any scratches made tend to show white, considerably detracting from the overall appearance of a piece, thereby affecting its value.

Some of the glazes utilised by Bernard Moore were supplied by Wenger's of Burslem; and the collector may come across proof- pieces of Moore's designs marked 'A F Wenger'. The pottery bodies may also be marked on the base with a variety of factory marks, indicating their origin.

**References**

*1) 'Bernard Moore Master Potter (1815-1935), by Aileen Dawson; pub. Richard Dennis, 1982.*

*2) Victoria & Albert Museum (George Salting Collection)*

*3) Plymouth City Museum & Art Gallery.*

| Type of Ware | Production | Quality | Availability |
|---|---|---|---|
| Flambé (red) pieces (signed) | Low | Good to Very Good | Scarce |
| Crystalline & other colours | Very Low | Good to Very Good | Rare |
| Figures | Low | Good to Very Good | Scarce |

**Marks**

| | | |
|---|---|---|
| Painted, printed or incised through the glaze | Bernard Moore * | 1905-15 |
| Impressed: | MOORE | 1905-15 |
| Impressed: | MOORE BROS * | |
| Painted or incised through the glaze: | BM (sometimes with two wavy lines underneath) | 1905-15 |

± year

*± 'England' or 'Made in England'

± Artist's mark

(NB: on flambé pieces the mark is often in red on red, and so difficult to see)

± factory mark from a variety of Potteries, but mainly Wedgwood & Mintons

# MORTLAKE POTTERY

## George Cox, Mortlake, London, SW14 (c.1910-1914)

Typical Wares: earthenwares

### Historical Background & Products

**There have been potteries at Mortlake since 1742, and most are well documented. Little is known, however, of George Cox's pottery established at Mortlake about 1910, although several well produced earthenware designs were created during the four short years or so of the pottery's existence.**

It is known that George Cox studied art at the Royal College of Art, and was particularly interested in pottery as an expression of art. 'The best in his (the Potter's) craft has been produced by men that were artists rather than chemists', he wrote in 1914, emulating Christopher Dresser's quote that 'it is the art which gives the value, and not the material'.

Certainly, the technology of ceramics was not ignored by Cox, as demonstrated by some of the glaze effects he utilised, and he was clearly interested in giving others instruction in all aspects of the potter's craft.

Vases seem to have been the main output of the pottery at Mortlake, which, together with jars and pitchers, were often fairly large in size. All were well thrown, and many had a monochrome decoration with smooth glazes.

Brown was a frequently used colour in overall decoration, but a pastel grey- blue was also widely used. The pottery body was quite thick, as were some of the glazes. Some fine crystalline glazes were produced alongside the more usual smooth glazes. Cox experimented widely with high temperature glazes, producing a range of effects.

In 1914, Cox left for America and took up a post as 'Instructor in Pottery and Modelling' at Teachers' College, Columbia University. He published a book the same year, entitled 'Pottery for Artists, Craftsmen & Teachers', which was a handbook for students and teachers alike, concerning the artistic creation of ceramics. In his book he shows his designs for figurines, such as 'Saint George'; but basically the book is an instruction manual with a strong artistic bias.

The pottery at Mortlake was fairly obscure, and little information is readily available about its operation. Kelly's Directory for 1911 lists Cox as being resident at 11, South Worple Way, and there are no entries after 1914, when he left for America.

Whether he produced any art wares in America is not clear, but it is known that he produced several industrial designs, such as ceramic facades for buildings.

The quality of the Mortlake ware is good, but its scarcity makes collection difficult.

**References**

*1) 'Pottery for Artists, Craftsmen & Teachers', by George J Cox, ARCA; pub. Macmillan New York, 1914.*

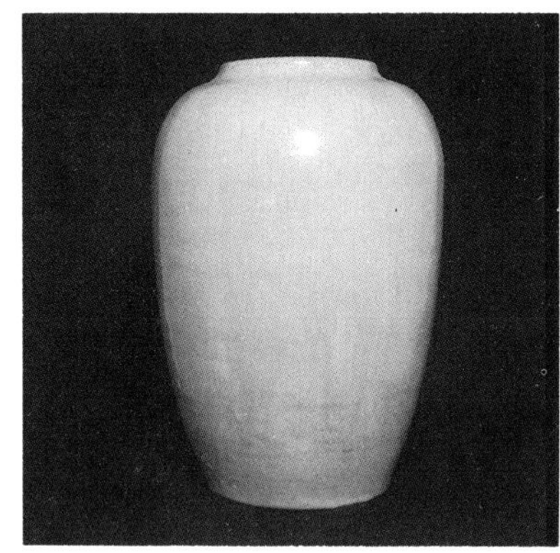

*Vase, 350 mm high, by George Cox.*

| Type of Ware | Production | Quality | Availability |
|---|---|---|---|
| Earthenwares | Very Low | Good | Scarce |

**Marks**

Incised: MORTLAKE (c.1910-1914)

± monogram of George Cox

± year

± monogram as part of the decoration:

± various artistic symbols, as part of the decoration.

# MYOTT & SON LTD. (1898-1986)

## Alexander Pottery, Stoke-on-Trent (1898- 1902)
## Cobridge, Staffs. (1902-1947)
## Hanley, Staffs. (1947- 1986)

Typical Wares: earthenware, moulded wares,

### Historical Background & Products

**In 1898, Myott & Son took over the Alexander Pottery at Stoke-on- Trent, which had been producing earthenware since 1880. The firm moved to Cobridge in 1902, then to Hanley in 1947.**

From the early 1900's, Myott & Sons were producing art pottery, often similar to Carlton Ware, but generally considered by collectors not to be of such high quality.

Many sets and combination pieces were produced, such as ewers and jugs, sandwich sets, candlesticks and dressing-table sets; and some pieces were moulded. The decorations tended to be bright and gaudy, such as large geometric patterns or exaggerated leaves in red, orange or black, often on a yellow-ochre ground. Shapes were usually simple, and much use was made of underglaze painting.

At the 1920 British Industrial Arts Exhibition, Myott & Son exhibited a bold blue-banded ware which was well thought of by visitors, as was an *Indian Tree* pattern (No. 6514). There is little detail at present, however, of the names of many of Myott & Son's other wares.

During the 1920's, some fine semi-porcelain tea and dinner sets were produced, as well as many toilet sets. Although the decorations tended to be bright, many of the designs were remarkably original, and, unlike Carlton Ware, Myott pieces generally exhibited a characteristic overall style.

During the 1930's, more exaggerated shapes were produced in an art deco style, such as fan-shaped vases. The Pottery Gazette describes Myott's decorations in the 1930's as being 'free colourful treatments, much in demand'.

*Tazza, crocus pattern, 220 mm diam., transfer printed mark in gold 'Myott, Son & Co., Made in England, Hand Painted' with pattern no. 9244. Chrome base.*

Prints and enamels were widely used on Myott's tableware designs during the 1930's, and the Company registered almost 500 different patterns between the years 1933 and 1935.

Typical of the Myott patterns of this period was a range for tableware decorated with pencilled bands, and a hand-painted decoration of autumn leaves touched up in silver and green. Modernistic designs were also produced, such as *Swallow* and *Acorn*, and a cubist pattern was launched in 1935, reminiscent of a checkered tablcloth, which was available in three colour schemes; green and black, orange and black, or blue.

Original shapes at this time included a 'Jubilee' cider set with cider jug, and a flying-saucer shaped posie bowl, available in three sizes.

| Type of Ware | Production | Quality | Availability |
|---|---|---|---|
| Earthenwares | High | Fair to Good | Abundant |

**Marks**

| | | |
|---|---|---|
| Printed:<br>(Usually in black but often in gold) | MYOTT, SON & CO<br>ENGLAND<br>(+ crown) | 1907 onwards |
| | M S & CO<br>ENGLAND<br>(+ crown) | 1900 onwards |

# OXSHOTT POTTERY (1920-present)

## Oakshade Road, Oxshott, Surrey (1920-1978)

### Typical Wares: earthenware, stoneware

## Historical Background

**The Oxshott Pottery was established in 1912 by Denise Tuckfield (later Wren), who had studied design at Kingston School of Art from 1907 under the direction of the designer and painter Archibald Knox (1864-1933).**

Knox was well-known for his revival of Celtic designs, designing many art nouveau pieces for Liberty & Co. in their 'Cymric' silver and 'Tudric' pewter ranges. His teaching at Kingston School of Art, however, was criticised as being too advanced, and he resigned his post in 1912, taking his student with him.

Many of his jewellery and silver designs were salvaged, and Denise's elder sister Winifred Tuckfield promptly established the Knox Guild of Design and Crafts at 24a, Kingston Market Place to accommodate his students. Denise established herself as a potter in the Guild rooms, whilst other members concentrated on jewellery making, embroidery, raffia work, spinning and weaving. Exhibitions were held in the Art Gallery above Kingston Library and at Whitechapel Art Gallery. Although the rooms were relinquished upon the outbreak of war, the Knox Guild continued to exhibit until the 1930's.

In 1915, Denise married Henry Wren, who had also been a student of Knox at Wimbledon School of Art.

In March, 1920, the Wren's purchased a plot of land at Oxshott on which they built an unusual bungalow to a design by Denise, naming it 'Potter's Croft'. The Knox Guild made various contributions to the furnishing of the interior through curtains and stained-glass.

Between 1925 and 1939, Denise designed many coke-fired kilns at Oxshott, the plans of which were regularly sold to other potters.

Students often came to the pottery for short courses, and Denise also undertook some teaching.

Pieces were exhibited at the British Empire Exhibition, Wembley in 1924 and 1925. Work was also taken to agricultural and horticultural shows, such as the Chelsea Flower Show. Both Denise and Henry also organised an exhibition of about thirty leading craftsmen at the Central Hall, Westminster in 1925, which ran annually every autumn until 1938, and was known as "The Artist Craftsman".

During the mid-1930's, Denise also designed textiles, some of which were sold at Liberty & Co.

Henry Wren died in 1947 but Denise carried on the pottery. Denise's daughter, Rosemary (b.1922) took over her father's workshop, and both Denise and Rosemary embarked on new pottery styles from then on.

The pottery moved to Devon in 1978, where Denise Wren died in 1979, aged 88.

## Products

The first wares produced at Oxshott were candlesticks, plates and vases.Some items were coiled, others thrown or press-moulded.

Between 1920 and 1939, decoration was primarily of animals or patterns created using cut and incised slips, or lines incised into the clay. Some slip-trailed decoration was also executed.

Designs and shapes tended to be simple, the influence of Knox's 'Celtic Art' often being evident.

Many pieces were undecorated, relying on shape and a single colour glaze (often blue, yellow, orange or green) for effect. However, the accentuated ridge effect created in the throwing frequently allowed the clay to show through the glaze.

Some interesting glaze effects were created through over-firing, such as an orange "stormy sunset" uranium glaze, or through high-firing, such as a turquoise "majolica" glaze.

From the mid-1920's, containers for flower arrangements were a popular product of the pottery, such that Denise Wren came to be known as "the producer of pots for flowers" (a theme which she was to develop later in her career (1958-1968) by making many pieces designed as containers for Japanese flower arrangements).

Some figures were also produced, notably "St. George and the Dragon" (1928).

After 1968, Denise Wren concentrated on making models of elephants, working until she was 84 years of age.

**References**

*1) 'The Oxshott Pottery' by Denise and Henry Wren, pub. Crafts Study Centre, 1984 * (catalogue of retrospective exhibition).*

*2) The Holburne Museum, Bath, has some Oxshott pieces, as well as photographs and records in their Crafts Study Centre.*

*3) The Museum and Heritage Centre, Kingston upon Thames, also has some pieces and early records.*

*4) Weybridge Museum, Weybridge, Surrey, has example of work post-1960, plus photographs, records and equipment from the early pottery.*

*5) Rosemary Wren continues the Oxshott Pottery with her partner Peter Crotty at Strathpeffer, Scotland, having moved from Devon in 1989.*

(Special thanks to Rosemary Wren for providing the bulk of the information for this chapter).

| Type of Ware | Production | Quality | Availability |
|---|---|---|---|
| Earthenwares (1920-1935) | Low | Fair | Scarce |

**Marks**

| | | | |
|---|---|---|---|
| Incised | OXSHOTT | 1920 - present | |
| ± incised initials: | | | |
| Henry Wren | HW | | 1920-1947 |
| Denise K Wren | DKW | | 1920-1975 |
| Denise K Wren | DKW (and bird) | (where space allowed) | 1920-1975 |
| Rosemary Wren | Bird impressed | | 1945-present |
| Rosemary Wren | Bird impressed 'Oxshott' | | 1950-c.1960 |
| (made by Rosemary Wren, and decorated by Peter Crotty | Bird impressed + monogram for Peter Crotty | | 1979-present |

# PILKINGTON TILE & POTTERY CO.

## Clifton Junction, Manchester (1892-1938)

Typical Wares: earthenware, lustres, tiles

### Historical Background

**In 1892, Pottery Studios were opened at Clifton Junction, Manchester, subsidised by the Pilkington Glass Company. They were set up to produce quality wares, and top designers were employed for this purpose.**

William Burton was appointed manager of the Company in 1893. He had previously worked for Wedgwood as a chemist, and was interested in glaze effects, as was his friend Bernard Moore.

From 1893 to 1897, tiles were the main output of the firm, and from 1897 to 1903, the decoration (but not production) of art pottery was undertaken. The Company maintained a high standard of decoration and rejected pieces of inferior quality.

Some of the tiles were decorated under commission by well-known artists, such as Lewis F Day and Charles Annesley Voysey, whilst spectacular lustrewares were designed by the artists Walter Crane and W S Mycock, and decorated by competent artists such as Richard Joyce and Charles E Cundall.

William Burton's brother, Joseph, joined the firm in 1895. He became managing director of the Company, and according to the Pottery Gazette was the guiding light in the years to come.

In 1903, a potter's wheel was installed, and pottery was thrown as well as decorated. A good pottery thrower by the name of Edward Thomas Radford was engaged (remaining until 1936), and in 1906, the artist Gordon Forsyth joined the firm, contributing significantly to the production of lustre-painted wares in the following years.

The Paris Exhibition of 1900 influenced greatly the production of lustreware, and Pilkington launched their first range in 1903. The lustres were a technically difficult process, and because of the high cost of production, output was relatively low.

In 1913, Pilkington's lustreware became known as Royal Lancastrian lustreware, though lustres were not the only type of pottery to be produced under this mark. The Royal Lancastrian wares continued until well into the 1920's, and included such styles as Gwladys Rodgers' Lapis Ware (from 1928).

William Burton retired in 1915, and in 1919 Forsyth left Pilkington's to become Principal of Stoke-on-Trent Schools of Art (although in spite of this loss Pilkington continued to produce lustrewares until 1927).

Richard Joyce died in 1931, and Joseph Burton died in 1935. When Edward Radford retired in 1936 it seemed that production of the art wares could hardly continue through the loss of so many people important to their production.

The last firing at the pottery of art wares was in March 1938, the directors having decided that because of the trade depression they could not bring themselves to manufacture cheaper wares of lower quality. As Pilkington Tiles Ltd. the Company continued to produce tiles, merging with the Poole Pottery in 1964.

The Royal Lancastrian Pottery was revived, however, for a short period from 1948 to 1957, when wares were produced designed by William Barnes, and thrown by John Brannan and Eric Bridges who had worked at the pottery before the War.

For another short period (1972-1975) a

*Vase, 120 mm high, uranium glaze, by Richard Joyce, marked 'Royal Lancastrian ENGLAND'.*

revival attempt of old pottery styles was made by Pilkington's at Blackpool under the name 'Lancastrian Pottery'. Pilkington Tiles Ltd. continue to produce tiles today.

## Products

Some pottery was manufactured with pressed and cast shapes in 1897, but thrown wares were only produced from 1903. The early wares were sometimes decorated with flecked or crystalline glazes developed by the chemist Abraham Lomax.

In 1903, William Burton developed a range of scarlet and tangerine orange glazes using uranium. This latter became known as *uranium orange*, which developed into *orange vermilion* (an orange glaze with red specks). Together with the matt glaze *ultramarine blue* (later known as *Kingfisher blue*) these glazes led to the development of the celebrated lustrewares, which encompassed a wide range of brilliant colours, in particular ruby and silver lustres.

Mostly vases, bottles and plates were produced as lustrewares, but up to 1914 some excellent smaller items were also produced, such as circular boxes and trays.

Some decoration was in the classical style, such as tall covered vases with Grecian or Egyptian scenes, the outline often being depicted in silver lustre on a red or blue ground, with a crazed underglaze. Other pieces were decorated with animal scenes, or heraldic devices with Gothic lettering, depending of the speciality of the artist.

Richard Joyce decorated some fine vases with fish scenes on a dark green ground, and many of the Pilkington lustrewares exhibit this characteristic of detail against a dark background. Richard Joyce also modelled animals and birds with lustre decoration.

The lustre plates tend to be heavy and deep, with internal ribbing much in evidence, but shapes were kept simple, the main impact being that of the decoration.

Generally, the lustres were glazed all over, such that there is no indication of the pottery body below. This often gives the appearance of pieces being made out of glass rather than pottery.

Vases were also produced in non-lustre glazes, and about 1911, designs included short-necked bases (after the Ruskin style) in streaked monochrome glazes, sometimes revealing the red body beneath. Some flambé wares were also produced, but these are scarce.

Complete picture panels of tiles were produced both for floors, walls and fireplaces. Lewis Day produced several Persian scenes, as did the designer John Chambers. Walter Crane's tile designs often featured female figures in floreate surrounds, whilst Voysey frequently concentrated on bird and leaf studies. Some nursery themes were produced on tiles, notably a series of nursery rhymes designed by Margaret Pilkington using tube-line decoration.

From 1927, tiles and pottery were also decorated with mottled effect matt glazes, produced using titanium oxide.

In 1928, Gwladys M Rodgers, a painter at Pilkington, worked on a series of *Lapis Ware*. This consisted of pieces with a smooth matt feldspathic glaze (similar to that of Poole) and abstract decoration in pastel streaks of blue, green or grey. The decoration is either plain or representative of foliage; and although the ware tends to be rather unassuming, it is none the less individual in style.

About the same period, further interesting non-lustre glazes were evolved. An all matt black glaze was produced for bottle-like vases and jugs (similar to Wedgwood's 'Basalt Ware'), and W S Mycock decorated some heavy plates bearing an orange Cadmium glaze.

The quality of the later wares is somewhat variable, although artist signed pieces were always of good quality at Pilkington. Some rather nondescript domestic items were produced during the 1930's, often resembling Keith Murray's designs for Wedgwood but with a mass-produced appearance.

The lustrewares, however, are by far the most impressive of the Pilkington Pottery's output, commanding high prices at auction; and Walter Crane's designs are especially sought after by collectors. The quality and artistry of these wares have rarely been equalled amongst modern ceramists, even though some exceiting achievements have been made in modern lustres to date.

**References**


1) *Manchester City Art Gallery.*

2) *'Pilkington Royal Lancastrian Pottery & Tiles' by A J Cross; pub. Richard Dennis, 1980.*

3) *'Royal Lancastrian Pottery 1900-1938' by Abraham Lomax; pub. privately, 1957.*

4) *'Pilkington's Royal Lancastrian Pottery 1904-1957'; article by A J Cross in The Antique Dealer & Collector, September, 1973.*

5) *'The Royal Lancastrian Pottery'; article by Tony L Mortimer in the journal of the Antiques Collectors' Club, September, 1985.*

6) *'Pilkington's Royal Lancastrian Lustre Pottery'; article by Lynne Thornton in The Connoisseur, May 1970.*


| Type of Ware | Production | Quality | Availability |
|---|---|---|---|
| Tiles (artist signed) | Low | Good to Very Good | Scarce |
| Lustrewares (pre-1914) | Low | Excellent | Scarce |
| Lustrewares (post-1914) | Low | Good to Excellent | Uncommon |
| Other art wares | Low to moderate | Good to Very Good | Common (certain varieties scarce) |

**Marks**

Pilkinton's pottery is well marked, the mark often being a work of art in itself. Sometimes it is incorporated in a small scene on the base of a piece, depending on the artist. On plates and large based items, the base is often of a different decoration.Nearly all Pilkington pieces bear the characteristic three point kiln marks on the base.

| | | |
|---|---|---|
| Incised: | P (in italics) | c.1900 |
| Impressed: | P (with bees) | 1901-1904 |
| | ( ± ENGLAND) | 1905-1914 |

+ year in Roman Numerals (eg. VI = 1906)
P (with Tudor rose)
ROYAL LANCASTRIAN 1914-1938

± Artist's mark:-

| | |
|---|---|
| Richard Joyce (c.1904-1931) (animals and fishes, particularly) | : 'JR' in monogram |
| Gordon Forsyth (1906-1919) (lettering and heraldry, particularly) | : Circular arrangement of four scythes |
| Charles Cundall (1907-1914) (peacocks, deer, particularly) | : 'CEC' in monogram |
| William Mycock (1894-1938) (galleons, particularly) | : 'WSM' in monogram |
| Lewis F Day | : 'LFD' in monogram |
| Gwladys Rodgers (c.1907-1938) (Lapis Ware, particularly) | : 'R' in shield |
| Walter Crane animals, flowers, female figures, galleons, etc | : 'CW' and crane bird in monogram |
| Edmund Kent (1910-1939) | : 'EK' in monogram |
| John Spencer (1936-1938) | : 'JLS' in monogram |
| Dorothy Dacre (to c.1908) | : 'DD' in monogram |
| John Chambers | : 'JC' in monogram |
| Jessie Jones (to c.1909) | : reversed J's in thistle in monogram |
| Albert Barlow (from 1903) | : 'AB' in monogram |
| Albert Hall | : 'AH' in monogram |
| Thomas Evans (1894-1935) | : 'TE' in monogram |

± Artists's year code:-

| | | |
|---|---|---|
| eg 1) William Mycock: | fleur de lis motif | 1914 |
| | crossed swords | 1915 |
| | floral circlet | 1916 |

1928 1929
1930 1931
1932 1933
1934 1935
1936 1937

| | | |
|---|---|---|
| 2) Gordon Forsyth: | flaming torch motif | 1914 |
| | bird passant gardant | 1915 |
| | swan | 1916 |
| | pair of wings | 1919 |
| 3) Richard Joyce: | sickle and corn | 1914 |
| | a fish | 1915 |
| | a lyre | 1916 |
| | a cross | 1917 |
| | 'R' in circle | 1918 |
| | a crown | 1919 |

± Thrower's mark:-

| | | |
|---|---|---|
| Incised: | E.T.R | Edward Thomas Radford (common on post 1928 wares) |

# POOLE POTTERY

## Poole, Dorset (1873-present)

### Typical Wares: earthenware, tiles, modelled items

## Historical Background

**In 1873, the East Quay Works at Poole was acquired by Jesse Carter, who, utilising the local deposit of Dorset Ball Clays, set about producing floor tiles for the domestic market.**

*Carter's Red* floor tiles soon became well established, such that by the end of 1883, production was supplemented by the making of glazed, modelled and painted wall tiles.

About this time, Jesse Carter was assisted by his two sons, Charles and Owen, and in 1895, Carter purchased the Architectural Pottery at nearby Hamworthy for the production of architectural faience and floor tiles.

In 1908, Carter & Co. became Carter & Company Limited. The pottery premises were expanded along the quay, taking the form of bottle kilns and workshops, which survived until 1945. A new factory was constructed at Hamworthy specifically for the production of white and cream wall tiles.

When Jesse Carter retired, Owen Carter took over the running of the pottery. Owen was a close friend of William De Morgan and William Burton, both pioneers of art pottery in their own right. Until his death in 1919, Owen tried to emulate their work, producing lustre glazed ware in a reducing kiln. This was the beginning of art pottery as such at Poole, and in 1912 the Poole (East Quay) works became the centre of studio work in the Carter Group of Companies, the other works concentrating on domestic and architectural ware.

With the decline in the tile trade at the outbreak of war in 1914, a specialised production of pottery buttons and beads was commenced, with limited amounts of lustre ware.

As the output of Owen Carter's 'Handcraft Pottery' increased, so did the employment of women artists, who were encouraged to produce their own patterns and attend evening classes at Poole Art School.

After the First World War, the London Stores of Liberty and Heals sold pieces (as did many local retailers), and the ware was advertised as 'suitable for country cottages and bungalows'. So much interest was aroused over the manufacture of the ware that about 1920, the works were made open to visitors.

Upon Owen Carter's death in 1919, Charles Carter invited the well known gold and silversmith Harold Stabler to advise him. Harold and his wife Phoebe, were accomplished ceramic modellers, and contributed much to the style of Poole Pottery from this time. In 1920, Harold introduced John Adams to the factory who had been a painter in Bernard Moore's pottery Studio; and in 1921, the company of Carter Stabler & Adams was formed.

By 1922, the workforce had doubled from that of two years ago, and Poole Pottery was in popular demand. The firm exhibited in Paris in 1925, and annually at the British Industries Fair.

In 1936, the first tableware sets were produced, and domestic production of quality pottery took a major step forward. Harold Stabler died in 1944 but the pottery continues today, with a craft section that is vigorously alive, and carrying on the fine tradition and principles that Owen Carter set many years before.

In 1963, the Company officially changed its name from Carter Stabler & Adams to Poole Pottery Limited, although it had been known unofficially as Poole Pottery since at least 1914. In 1964, Carter & Co Ltd merged into Pilkington Tiles Ltd.

## Products

Owen Carter developed the production of tube-line tiled panels, together with a form of mosaic and modelled majolica ware. His experimental ware of the First World War consisted of vases, tiles, bowls, dishes and candlesticks with lustre glazes, both plain and decorated, glazed and unglazed.

In 1914, a skilled thrower by the name of Radley Young was appointed works designer at Poole. He produced a series of beaker vases, bowls, jam pots, and butter dishes in a buff vitreous body, with a decoration in brown of geometric lines, which gave the ware a Neolithic appearance. This design proved popular, and by the end of 1915 a new ware had been launched, consisting of items with a reddish body, coated with grey or cream slip, and having a tin glaze. Again, geometric patterns were used, and were painted over the glaze in pastel shades of blue, yellow, pink and green, such that on firing the colours fused into the glaze. This process is still used today in producing Poole Pottery.

The Carter Stabler & Adams partnership concentrated strictly on Studio pottery at the East Quay Works, and it was Truda Carter who introduced the traditional style of Poole Pottery familiar to most collectors. Production of Owen Carter's lustre ware was quickly dropped, and the traditional designs of multi-coloured geometric patterns on a cream or white ground, with or without the famous *blue-bird* design, were quickly launched. The glaze was silky in finish, smooth to the touch and thin in consistency.

The *blue-bird* design became the hallmark of Poole Pottery for many years, the *blue-bird* often acompanied by a dazzle of multicoloured swirls and stylised flower-heads. Generally, the overall colour effect was mauve, though subtle greens, reds and yellows were also present in the design.

Vases, bowls and jugs, bearing the *blue-bird* design were produced mainly in either simple or classical shapes. Occasionally, the decoration misfired, and the collector will notice pieces with patchy or broken-up decoration.

*Selection of wares. l to r:- i) bowl, 200 mm diam., monochrome decoration, ii) vase, 175 mm high, 'bluebird' decoration. iii) early bowl, 175 mm diam.*

During the early 1920's, John Adams launched some special colour glazes, with names such as *Chinese Blue*, *Vellum White*, *Zulu Black*, *Sylvan* and *Tangerine*, which were used to decorate ash-trays, candlesticks, vases and bowls. Some modelled items were produced, such as animals and fish, which were decorated in monochrome or two-tone colours.

A nursery toilet-set decorated with medallions of birds, fish and animals was particularly attractive. Following the success of the experimental glazed and unglazed pottery produced cheaply during the First World War, several other designs quickly followed into the 1920's. A series of *Portuguese* designs based on the earlier styles was launched, decorated with a predominantly dull blue stripe on a brownish earthenware ground.

In 1920, a range of semi-dull green ware was produced with a simple decoration in black, entitled *Monastic Ware*, but the main product of the 1920's was the tradional multicoloured style that has become a hallmark for collectors.

About 1925, John Adams' *Persian Stag* design appeared, and in this style the geometric patterns were often punctuated with animal or floral motifs. Some modelling was also undertaken by John Adams, and items such as small trays and vases were modelled in part (usually the handles).

A range of figures was produced by Phoebe Stabler, but these are rare. Harold and Phoebe Stabler also designed and modelled facades for buildings and monuments, which were marketed as 'Constructional Della Robbia', and included commissions such as portions for a War Memorial at Rugby School.

E E Strickland, working about 1925 to 1930, produced a *Farmyard* series of tiles (pattern code FY4) using printed patterns of turkeys, hens and other farm animals.

During the late 1920's, the red body of the wares was replaced by a cream body, which was supplied from Carter's tile works.

In 1935, the *Sylvan* series was launched, characterised by broken colour effects on a matt glaze. Floreate designs with swirls and geometric lines were executed in brown, yellow and grey, and green, blue and grey, in particular. In the same year, a range of nursery ware was produced, designed by Dora Batty.

For collectors, certain individual lines of Poole art ware are rare, but as a general rule Poole wares are widely disseminated. Quality is good and prices, at the time of writing, are reasonable. The pottery is still somewhat underrated on the antiques market at present.

**References**

1) *The Poole Pottery no longer welcomes visitors round the works, but there is a small museum of early wares and a large shop selling current creations. Some pottery making demonstrations are put on for visitors.*

2) *The Poole Potteries, by Jennifer Hawkins; pub. Barrie & Jenkins, 1980.*

3) *Poole Pottery - The First 100 Years, by Jo McKeown; pub. Poole Pottery, 1973.*

4) *'The Poole Potteries'; catalogue of an Exhibition at the Victoria & Albert Museum, London, 1978; pub. V & A.*

5) *'The Potters of Poole', by Graham Crossingham- Gower; article in Art & Antiques, March 22nd, 1975.*

| Type of Ware | Production | Quality | Availability |
|---|---|---|---|
| Early art pieces (except tiles) | Low to Moderate | Poor to Good | Scarce |
| Lustres and reduced glazes | Low | Good | Rare |
| Pieces from 1921 | Moderate to High | Good to very Good | Common |
| Pieces from 1925 | High | Fair to Good | Abundant |
| Tiles | High to very High | Good | Common |

**Marks**

|  |  | |  |
|---|---|---|---|
| Incised, Impressed or Printed: | Carter Poole | | 1873-1921 |
| | Carter Co Poole | | 1873-1921 |
| | CARTERS POOLE (within concentric circles, with dolphin in centre). | | 1873-1921 |
| Impressed: | CARTER STABLER ADAMS ——— POOLE ENGLAND | (within lozenge) | 1921-1925 |
| | (the above + 'Ltd') | | 1925 - c. 1935 |
| Impressed or printed: | POOLE ENGLAND | (within lozenge) | 1921-1952 |

# EDWARD RADFORD (artist/potter) (b.1883; d.1968)

## Alexandra Pottery, Burslem (c.1920-1930) and Radford Handcraft Pottery, Amicable Street, Burslem (c.1930- c.1939)

Typical Wares: earthenware

### Historical Background

**Edward Thomas Brown Radford was the son of a skilled pottery thrower, Edward Thomas Radford (ref. Pilkington Tile & Pottery Co.). He worked initially for the Pilkington Pottery as a thrower, like his father before him, then as a salesman, and after the Great War joined H J Wood Ltd. in Burslem as a designer/salesman, managing his own Studio.**

About the year 1930, he left H J Wood to work as a sales representative for other potteries before establishing his own business in Burslem as the Radford Handcraft Pottery. This enterprise probably continued until the Second World War, producing hand-painted decorative wares.

After the war, Radford left Burslem to run a church holiday home with his wife. He died in 1968.

### Products

Mostly vases were produced, generally of simple shape, but with decoration varying from sgrafitto (*Sgraffiato Ware*) to hand-painted. Radford's glazes were thin with a smooth finish, the colours being fused into the glaze, similar to the process at Poole. The general style is of soft, delicate decorative lines on thickly potted shapes, and many pieces exhibit a restrained art deco approach, both in shape and decoration.

As for decoration, floral subjects were predominant, foxgloves, lupins and anemones being popular. Abstract patterns involving bands of colour were also used, but art deco geometric designs were not amongst the principal forms of decoration used, the floral patterns being more typical.

*Vase, 125 mm high, stamped 'E.Radford, Burslem' with pattern no. 8/F.*

The flowers depicted were decorated in pastel colours, such as mauve, blue or pink, mostly on a honey coloured ground. Some mottled backgrounds were also used, such as pastel green or pink. Apparently, the paintresses would often work from bunches of real flowers or designs on seed packets.

The pottery body is white, and is usually revealed on the base of pieces. The quality of throwing was good, as was the decoration and glaze.

Decorative motifs tended to be simple and uncluttered,and often well suited to a functional purpose; for example, a tall lupin decorated vase for lupins and an African violet plant-pot for an African Violet plant!

Shapes were chosen for their simplicity, and ranged from typically art deco reversed cone vases to tall, slim ewers, posy holders and Grecian style bowls.

Ware marked 'Sgraffiato Ware' tended to consist of incised floral motifs, such as leaf patterns, with a single outline colour under a smooth glaze, reminiscent of the *Lapis Ware* thrown by Radford's father at Pilkington's.

**References**

*1) Northern Ceramics Society Newsletter No. 36, December 1979, by Maureen Leese.*

| Type of Ware | Production | Quality | Availability |
|---|---|---|---|
| All wares | Moderate to High | Good to Very Good | Abundant |

**Marks**

| | | |
|---|---|---|
| Printed in black: (at Radford Handcraft Pottery) | E. Radford (in signature) Burslem | c.1930-c.1939 |
| Printed: (at H J Wood Ltd.) | E. Radford England Hand painted | c.1920 to present* |

± name of ware, eg 'Sgraffiato Ware'

* Apparently, H J Wood Ltd. continue to use this backstamp today for wares decorated in the Radford Studio, but not necessarily designed by E Radford.

# CHARLOTTE RHEAD - Artist/Decorator (b.1885; d.1947)

Typical Wares: earthenwares

## Historical Background

**Charlotte Rhead was the daughter of the renowned ceramic designer, Frederick Rhead. Born in 1885 she started her pottery career decorating tiles at the firm of T & R Boote in Burslem. Here she learned the art of tube-line decoration, which was to be her hallmark in later years.**

In 1913, she moved to Wood & Sons Ltd where her father had been made Art Director in 1912. Both Harry Wood and Frederick Rhead were keen on promoting art wares and in 1920 a separate company, Bursley Ltd, at the Crown Pottery, Burslem, was formed specifically for this purpose.

Charlotte Rhead moved to the Crown Pottery, continuing with her tube-lining, whilst her father concentrated on table-wares. She also did work for an associate firm, Ellgreave Pottery Co. Ltd.

In 1926 Charlotte moved to Burgess & Leigh at the Middleport Pottery, Burslem, in order to train a team of tube-liners. The practice of tube-lining, or the squeezing of wet clay from a rubber bag to form raised tubular lines, was an immense success. It was a form of decoration that could be freely and easily applied, as opposed to the more costly and time consuming pâte-sur-pâte method.

Burgess & Leigh produced many of their art wares under the title 'Burleigh Ware'. Some pieces were sold through the retail outlet of Lawley's, and contain the mark 'Lawley's Norfolk Pottery Stoke.'

From 1931 to 1943, Charlotte worked for A G Richardson in Cobridge, who manufactured Crown Ducal Ware. Initially, Richardson's premises were at the Gordon Pottery, Tunstall, but in 1934 the Britannia Pottery at Cobridge was acquired and rebuilt to modern standards.

Charlotte's designs were copied by the teams of decorators using a method known as 'pouncing'. This consisted of producing a pattern on paper outlined with pin-prick holes. The paper was placed on the pot and charcoal rubbed over the pattern, leaving an outline on the pot in charcoal which could be decorated.

In 1943, Charlotte left Richardson's and joined the firm of H J Wood Ltd, an associate company of Wood & Sons. Harry Wood set aside a part of the Alexandra Pottery, Burslem, for her to continue her tube line work and experiment in lustre glazes. Her death in 1947 cut short her experiments in this field.

**CHARLOTTE RHEAD**

**Wood & Sons Ltd., Burslem (1913-1920)**

**Bursley Ltd, Crown Pottery, Burslem (1920-1926)**

**Burgess & leigh, Burslem (1926-1931)**

**A. G. Richardson, Cobridge (1931-1943)**

**H.J. Wood Ltd., Alexandra Pottery, Burslem (1943-1947)**

*Charger, 370 mm diam., foxglove tube-line decoration, marked 'Crown Ducal', '4953'.*

*Charger, 315 mm diam., green dragon tube-line decoration, 'Manchu' pattern, marked 'C. Rhead' with Crown Ducal mark.*

## Products

Charlotte Rhead's products range from large plates to small bowls and hollow electric lamp bases. Much of her decoration is of characteristic style, being tube-line and 'stitch' decoration on heavy-bodied wares. The 'stitch' decoration was often applied around the edge of pieces, and on some the whole surface was worked, giving a textured appearance.

Her colours tended to be pastel shades, often of pink or pinky- brown. A favourite decoration of plates and vases was of falling leaves in a rust brown colour on a pale background, and generally fruit and floral motifs were predominant.

Charlotte's most renowned designs were executed between 1931 and 1943 when she worked for A G Richardson. Various standard patterns are recognisable, such as *Palermo*, a simple decoration resembling the head of a globe artichoke; *Manchu*, an oriental dragon motif; *Persian Rose*; *Foxglove*; *Wisteria*; *Byzantine*; *Pomegranite*; and *Hydrangea*.

Sometimes the decoration was effected on simple shaped vases or chargers, other times on pieces with a pronounced deco style of ribbed and stepped vases, mugs and jugs, often with multiple handles.

At H S Wood Ltd, a Trellis pattern was popular on plates, whilst a pattern of oranges and leaves was popular on vases and jugs. There is a noticeable increase in the use of lustres on the later pieces, which exhibit a silky shine as a result.

| **Type of Ware** | **Production** | **Quality** | **Availability** |
|---|---|---|---|
| All wares | Moderate to high | Good to Excellent | Abundant |

**Marks**

| | | | |
|---|---|---|---|
| 1 | Printed | Bursley Ware<br>England | c.1921-c.1929 |
| | Ellgreave Pottery Co Ltd<br>Lottie Rhead ware<br>Burslem<br>England | | c.1923 |
| 2 | Painted signature: | L Rhead (Lottie Rhead) | c.1926 - 1931 |
| | ± name of Pottery | | |
| | ± name of Ware (printed) | | |
| | eg Bursley Ware<br>Lottie Rhead Ware<br>Burleigh Ware | } | c.1926-1931 |
| | Lawley's Norfolk Pottery, Stoke | | c.1927 - 1930 |
| | ± decorator's marks and pattern numbers | | |
| 3 | Painted signature: | C Rhead | 1931 - 1943 |
| | ± Crown Ducal<br>Made in England (printed) | | c1931 - c.1938 |
| 4 | Printed mark: | Bursley Ware<br>Charlotte Rhead<br>England | c.1943 - c.1960 |
| 5 | Printed mark: | Wood's Arabesque<br>by<br>Charlotte Rhead | c.1943-1960 |

## Collecting Charlotte Rhead Pottery

Charlotte Rhead's creations are much admired by collectors of art deco. The style is very individual, and the lines are soft-textured with a certain solidarity, against warm tones of decoration.

Whilst there are bold patterns, the colours are rarely gaudy as in the wares of Clarice Cliff, and the pottery body is often similar to and as good as Poole pottery in quality and glaze. An interesting balance is thus achieved between decoration, shape and body, which is somewhat rare in art pottery of this period.

Refer to the numerous publications by Bernard Bumpas for detailed information on the confusing array of marks available.

**References**

*1) Charlotte Rhead, Potter & Designer, by Bernard Bumpas; pub. Kevin Francis, 1988.*

*2) 'Rhead Artists & Potters 1870-1950', Catalogue of an Exhibition at the Geffrye Museum, London, 1986, by Bernard Bumpas (touring exhibition).*

*3) 'Cheerful Charlotte Rhead'; article by Bernard Bumpas in The Antique Dealer & Collector, August 1988.*

*4) 'Pottery Designed by Charlotte Rhead'; article by Bernard Bumpas in The Antique Collector, January 1983.*

*5) 'Tube-Line Variations'; article by Bernard Bumpas in The Antique Collector, December, 1985.*

# THE RUSKIN POTTERY

## West Smethwick, Birmingham (1898 - 1933)

Typical Wares: earthenware, flambé & Sang-de-boeuf, lustre and crystalline glazes

### Historical Background

**The Ruskin Pottery was established by Edward Richard Taylor and his son William Howson Taylor in 1898, and was named after the artist John Ruskin. Many art pieces were produced, and the company enjoyed much success at international exhibtions (see below).**

With the help of Wedgwood craftsmen, the Taylors experimented in high temperature glazes and lustres, the recipes of which were kept a closely guarded secret. Apparently, William Howson Taylor destroyed his notes when he retired from the pottery in 1933.

The glazes, moreover, were much admired, and the flambe glaze won a prize at the St Louis Centennial Exhibition in 1904. Other notable prizes were won at Milan, and in New Zealand, and the pottery exhibited pieces at the British Industrial Art Exhibition in 1920.

Praise came from all quarters and the pottery was patronised by Queen Victoria and members of the Royal Family.

Edward Richard Taylor died in 1913. His son, however, carried on the business, and became the guiding influence on the products that we see and admire today. Howson Taylor maintained meticulous standards with his ware and no 'seconds' were allowed to be sold. Seconds were either destroyed or given to the workforce for personal use.

The potter Bernard Leach was a frequent visitor to the pottery, and also a personal friend of Howson Taylor. The two pottery styles, however, could not have been more diverse, but Leach must have been greatly interested in the Ruskin *oriental* shapes and glazes.

Ill health forced Howson Taylor to close the pottery in December 1933, and having retired to Devon with his wife, he died in September 1935.

### Products

By far the most interesting of the pottery's products are the high temperature glazes. Some fine vases and bowls of simple shape were produced, decorated with coloured speckles in a matt finish, or with interesting flambé and sang-de-boeuf glazes.

Flambé pieces were often speckled with viridian spots, which were produced by the use of copper salts. Howson-Taylor also produced a *souffle ware* (which consisted of a mottled glaze in a single colour), various crackle glazes; and, from 1929, some crystalline glazes.

The mottled glazes were produced in many different colours; greys, celadons, dark blues, greens, mauves and pinks. Often the glaze itself was the only decoration, but on some pieces plant forms were painted on a coloured ground. Of the lustres, predominant were a pink lustre, and a pearl lustre with a kingfisher blue glaze.

The high-fired pieces were more heavily potted than the normally fired pieces, and were produced using a Cornish clay, obtained through A. F. Wenger, the clay and glaze suppliers. Presumably, the thinly-potted pieces produced using a local clay would not withstand the high temperatures of the kiln.

A special kiln known as the 'Secret Red Kiln' was used to fire the flambe and sang-de-boeuf pieces, the colour being achieved by firing a copper glaze in 'reducing' conditions.

The vases decorated with flambé and sang-de-boeuf glazes tended to be Chinese inspired. Some had covers and even specially produced stands. Other items made included egg-cups, bowls, jars, candlesticks, lamp bases, ink-pots, brooches, cuff-links and hat- buttons; and some pieces were mounted in silver. The collector will occasionally come across trade samples, rather like domed brooch centres in appearance.

From the early 1920's, a cheaper moulded ware was produced in answer to the demand from those who could not afford the fairly expensive high-fired pieces.

### Collecting Ruskin Pottery

There has been a surge of interest recently amongst dealers and collectors over the Ruskin high-fired wares. Prices have been extremely high at auction, and been rather out-of-line with the high quantity of pieces produced. The high temperature wares are not rare, but generally all are of good quality. The pink lustres are extremely attractive, though not as bright as the Pilkington lustres, or as matt as the De Morgan lustres.

The bulbous shapes and small necks of the orientally-inspired vases exhibit a pleasing symmetry. The mottled pieces have a chunky appearance with a smooth matt finish, and on other pieces the pottery body sometimes has an egg-shell like appearance, with the hardness of stoneware, but with the thinness of porcelain. Certainly, Ruskin pottery is widely collected and sought after, and there will always be a ready market for it.

**References**

*1) A collection of Ruskin pottery was presented by Howson Taylor to the County Borough of Smethwick, and may be seen at the Central Library, High Street, Smethwick.*

*2) Ruskin Pottery, by James H Ruston - Metropolitan Borough of Sandwell, 1975.*

*3) 'Ruskin Pottery and the European Ceramic Revival'; catalogue of an Exhibition at Fernyhough, 1981, by I. Bennet.*

*Examples of high-fired vases. l to r:- i) vase, 225 mm high, with blue speckled glaze, dated 1907. ii) vase, 240 mm high, with beige and pale mauve speckled glaze, dated 1906. iii) vase, 301 mm high, with sang-de-boeuf glaze, dated 1907.*

**Summary of Wares**

| | |
|---|---|
| Red Kiln | : Sang-de-boeuf rouge flambé and special colours with flecks. Heavily potted pieces. |
| Soufflé | : Single colour products, with marbled or mottled gradations. Thinly potted and representative of the majority of Ruskin output. |
| Eggshell | : Almost porcelain; lightweight and delicate pieces |
| Lustres | : Generally monochrome; hard lustre and soft lustre glazes, the latter tending to wear off. |
| Moulded wares | : Mass-produced, eg lamp-bases, candle-sticks, ink-pots, vases. Generally squared and angular shapes. |
| Egyptian Ware | : Vases, jugs and jardinères in a rather heavy Egyptian-inspired ware. |

| **Type of Ware** | **Quality** | **Production** | **Availability** |
|---|---|---|---|
| High-fired and lustre glazes | Moderate | Very Good to Excellent | Uncommon |
| Crystalline and crackle glazes | Low | Good to Excellent | Scarce |
| Moulded wares | Moderate | Good to Very Good | Common |
| Other art wares | Moderate | Good | Common |

**Marks**

| | | | |
|---|---|---|---|
| Impressed | RUSKIN | | 1899 -1904 |
| | RUSKIN<br>POTTERY<br>WEST SMETHWICK | (within oval) | 1904-1915 |
| | RUSKIN<br>ENGLAND | | 1904-1933* |
| | RUSKIN<br>MADE IN ENGLAND | | 1920 - 1933 |
| | RUSKIN | | 1899 -1904 |
| Printed: | W. Howson Taylor<br>RUSKIN<br>ENGLAND | | 1920 - 1933 |

± year (most pieces are dated)

± the signature 'W Howson Taylor' 1899 -1903

± HW/S/

NB:
1) Most of the early ware (1898 to 1904) was not marked.
2) An outline of scissors (painted underglaze or incised) was also used as an underglaze mark until 1920.

* The mark 'RUSKIN ENGLAND' impressed has been noted used in conjuction with the incised signature 'W Howson Taylor' with the date impressed (eg 1931)

# THE RYE POTTERY

## Bellevue Pottery, Ferry Road, Rye, Sussex (1869 to present)

Typical Wares: earthenware, miniatures

### Historical Background & Products

**The Rye Pottery had been established since 1808, when Frederick Mitchell formed a partnership with his father to produce decorative pottery.**

In 1869, Frederick took over the running of the pottery, which became known as Bellevue Pottery, and set about producing art wares. His earliest and most famous art pieces consisted of brown and green glazed jugs, bowls, vases, candlesticks, pilgrim bottles and flower-baskets, which came under the general title of *Sussex Rustic Ware*. Decoration was usually in the form of foliage and hops, the jug handles resembling tree branches.

The clay used was white, and pieces are characterised as being light in weight. The quality of potting was good, and all pieces exhibit a high glaze, a common feature of which was a mottling effect.

Frederick Mitchell died in 1875, and his wife took over the running of the business, producing pottery imitative of continental styles. Production of the Rustic Ware recommenced in 1882 when Frederick Mitchell's son, Frederick T Mitchell, joined the firm.

From this time, miniature vases and jugs were produced in simple classical shapes. Decoration was mostly in green, but sometimes in brown or more unusually in blue with white stripes. The miniatures were produced from a white clay body and had a high glaze. Many were not more than half an inch in height, and are simply marked 'Rye', scratched on the unglazed base.

Some lustre ware was also made, but production was limited to small items, and output was low.

F T Mitchell died in 1920, but the pottery continues today, having had various owners since then.

**References**


1) *'Sussex Pottery' by John Manwaring Baines; pub. Fisher Publications, 1980.*

2) *Lewes Museum at Anne of Cleves House, Southover High Street, Lewes, Susex, has some fine examples of Sussex Rustic Ware and Sussex Art Ware.*

3) *Rye Museum has examples of all the Rye kilns since medieval times.*

*Jug, 214 mm high, 'Sussex Rustic Ware', marked 'F.Mitchell'. (courtesy HCMS, DA 1978.37, 'Coysh Collection').*

| Type of Ware | Production | Quality | Availability |
|---|---|---|---|
| 'Rustic Ware' | Moderate | Fair | Uncommon |
| Other art wares | Low | Good | Scarce |
| Miniature art wares | Low to Moderate | Fair to Good | Uncommon |

**Marks**

| | | |
|---|---|---|
| Impressed or incised: | S / R W / RYE (crossed lines) | ('Sussex Rustic Ware') 1869 - 1920 |
| | S / A W / RYE (crossed lines) | ('Sussex Art Ware') 1920 - 1939 |
| Incised: | Rye | c. 1869 - 1939 |
| | Sussex Art Ware | 1920 - 1939 |
| | F.T.M. | Frederick T Mitchell |

# SALOPIAN ART POTTERY (1882-c.1920)

## Benthall Pottery Co., (1772-1982)
## Benthall, Broseley, Shropshire.

### Typical Wares: earthenwares

### Historical Background

**The Benthall Pottery was established in 1772 by John Thursfield, who had previously been producing stoneware at Jackfield nearby.**

The pottery went through various stages of ownership, merging with the Haybrook Pottery opposite in 1845. From this time, stoneware and brown 'Rockingham' wares were produced, and about 1862, the pottery came into the possession of the Allen family, and William Allen is recorded as being the manager from 1870 to 1907.

William Allen decided to venture into the production of art pottery, and in 1882 art wares were produced alongside the existing wares, though differentiated by the name 'Salopian Art Pottery'.

Little is known about the pottery or its products, even though a considerable variety of wares was produced. Jewitt records that almost 300 shapes were advertised in 1883, though many were 'ordinary yellow and other common wares'.

A local advertisement of 1882 boasts a variety of wares imitating classical styles (Egyptian, Grecian, etc.) and mentions a London agent as a retail outlet. The artist Francis Gibbons is also mentioned, and at least one vase has been found with his initials recorded on the base.

An unsuccessful attempt in 1907 by William Allen's son, William Beriah Allen, to send some of the pottery's employees to South Kensington School of Art led to the Company concentrating on the production of more domestic and industrial wares, such as electrical fittings and black lamp- bases, together with coarse terra-cotta wares, such as drain-pipes, garden ornaments and funerary items.

It seems, however, that art pottery was made on and off until about 1920, the Benthall Pottery Company continuing until 1982 with drain-pipes and other industrial items. The site today is used for the storage of agricultural machinery.

### Products

Local clays were used and pieces were made in both white and brown clays, occasionally mixed.

Glazes were primarily lead, thickish in consistency, but some early pieces were decorated with a tin glaze, and later wares had unleaded thin glazes.

The majority of wares were thrown, but some were press-moulded, slabbed and modelled.

The range of wares produced is amazing as are the similarities to other potteries' styles and designs. Given the diversity of styles it is possible, however, to group the art wares into recognisable types.

An early group of wares was known as *Rhodian* and consisted of brightly coloured painted decoration on a terra-cotta body with a tin glaze. Colours were predominantly yellow, but variations of the same designs were produced in different colours. The Rhodian range consisted of floreate designs around a stylised Cross of St. John and featured particularly well on large and small plates. This range is remarkably similar to some of Carlo Manzoni's designs for the Granville and Della Robbia Potteries, but almost certainly pre- dates these latter.

Another range of wares were advertised as 'barbotine' (compare Aller Vale Art Pottery) and featured thickly painted impasto decoration of recognisable flowers on a monochrome (often green) ground, and covered by a thick lead glaze. Vases featuring this form of decoration were similar to those produced at Aller Vale, though whether one influenced the other is difficult to say.

Another range produced was similar to the Aller Vale 'Scandy' pattern, and featured brightly coloured swirls similar in decoration to painted 'barge ware'. Some domestic items, such as coffee-pots were also produced in this pattern.

The Salopian wares, though similar to wares of other potteries, were often of a higher quality, and this is noticeable particularly with the Della Robbia and Aller Vale similarities.

A significant range of ware featured sgraffito work by the artist James Arthur Hartshorne, and bears some resemblance to Doulton's Silicon Ware. Precisely turned plant pots and jardinères were produced in a hard white or brown body, and featured a thin monochrome slip covering (usually blue), through which designs of birds, flowers, ferns and grasses were scratched. The quality of potting and decoration was good across this range, which was clearly designed to be functional as well as decorative.

Other wares featuring similarities to other potteries can be seen through gourd-shaped vases with streaked and mottled glazes similar to those designed by Christoper Dresser at Linthorpe, oriental glaze effects and shapes similar to Ruskin, and splashed and dribbled glazes similar to Bretby.

Many Salopian creations, however, were unique, such as the heavily modelled and brightly coloured clusters of fruit, either as centre pieces for table decoration or adorning flower baskets or jardinères. A large creation (for want of a better word!) may be seen displayed in the Clive House Museum, and features modelled terrapins and lizards.

**References**

*1) Jackfield Tile Museum, Jackfield, has some pieces.*

*2) Clive House Museum, Shrewsbury, has a good representative collection.*

*3) Ironbridge Gorge Museum archeaologists' reports.*

*Jardinère, 196 mm high, slab construction and press-moulded. (courtesy HCMS, 1972.599).*

*Selection of wares. l to r:- i) vase, 202 mm high, mottled glaze. ii) double gourd-shaped vase, 222 mm high, streaked glaze. iii) small vase, 109 mm high, 'Scandy' pattern. iv) coffee-pot and decorated stand, 235 mm high, 'Scandy' pattern.*

| **Type of Ware** | **Production** | **Quality** | **Availability** |
|---|---|---|---|
| Salopian art wares | Moderate (?) | Good to Very Good | Uncommon |

**Marks**

Most Salopian pottery is marked, the impressed mark often occurring near the base or on the foot of a piece.

| | | |
|---|---|---|
| Inscribed: | Salopian | 1882-c.1890? |
| ± name of ware, | eg. 'Rhodian 2B' | |
| Impressed: | SALOPIAN | 1882-c.1920 ? * |
| | SALOPIAN (within a diamond frame incorporating a butterfly and flower) | |
| Printed in black: | SALOPIAN (within a large diamond frame incorporating a butterfly and flower plus 'TRADE MARK' and 'ENGLAND') | c.1900?-c.1920? |
| | BENTHALL POTTERY BROSELEY | (in circle) |

*NB: Earlier porcelain wares from the Caughley factory used a similar mark.

# SHERWIN & COTTON

## Vine Street, Hanley, Staffs (1877-1911)

### Typical Wares: tiles

### Historical Background and Products

**Sherwin & Cotton produced mainly majolica tiles decorated with flowers, animals and portraits in relief.**

Colours were generally browns and greens, and the glazes high. The tiles were characterised by 'Sherwin's Patent Lock', a device designed so that the tiles could fit together more easily.

Portraits were the speciality of the firm and portrait tiles featured perosnalities such as Gladstone (1898), Abraham Lincoln (1909), General Booth of the Salvation Army (1904), Queen Victoria (1897), and many others, including two Maori chiefs (Tuari Netana and Matene Te Nga) and their Queens (Bella and Sophia).

The portraits were the work of George Cartlidge, who tended to work from photographs, although the tiles themselves were modelled to such fine detail that they were often thought to have been produced by a photographic process, particularly as many were also glazed in a deep sepia colour. Indeed the debate continues as to the exact method of production.

Cartlidge was a graduate of Hanley School of Art, and received his Art Master's Certificate in the same year that Sherwin & Cotton produced his first portrait tile, that of Queen Victoria in 1897. Other subjects modelled by Cartlidge on tiles include children, dogs and landscapes.

Although the portrait tiles were a successful venture, Sherwin & Cotton's Works closed in 1911. George Cartlidge managed to continue modelling tiles, however, and in 1916 he was engaged by J H Barratt & Co at the Boothen Works, Stoke. Here further portrait tiles were produced, including several of First World War personalities, such as Field Marshal Sir Douglas Haig, General Smuts and Admiral Sir John Jellicoe, and prime ministers, such as David Lloyd George, and U.S. presidents such as Abraham Lincoln.

Cartlidge continued to produce tiles for Barratt until about 1927, his later portraits extending to personalities of the Staffordshire Potteries, such as the sculptor Conrad Dressler, who worked at the Della Robbia Pottery for a time.

**References**

*1)'Photographic Portrait Tiles' by Eric Knowles; article in The Antique Collector, August, 1977.*

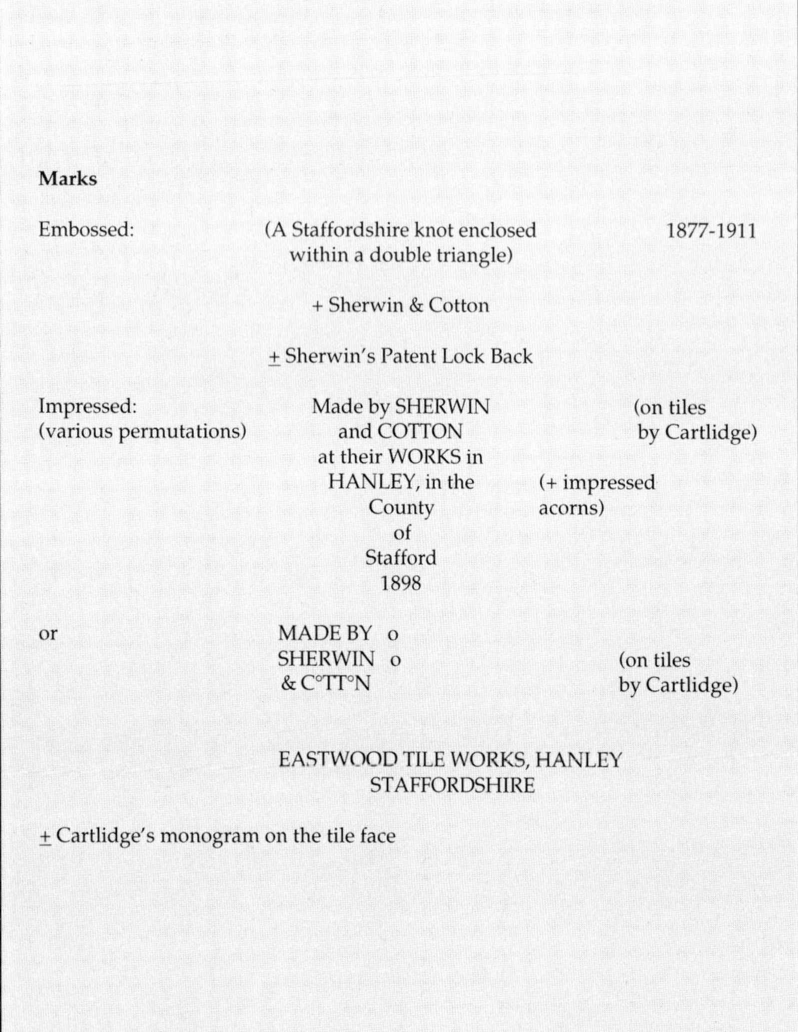

**Marks**

Embossed: (A Staffordshire knot enclosed within a double triangle) 1877-1911

+ Sherwin & Cotton

± Sherwin's Patent Lock Back

Impressed: (various permutations)
Made by SHERWIN
and COTTON
at their WORKS in
HANLEY, in the
County
of
Stafford
1898
(+ impressed acorns)
(on tiles by Cartlidge)

or
MADE BY o
SHERWIN o
& C°TT°N
(on tiles by Cartlidge)

EASTWOOD TILE WORKS, HANLEY
STAFFORDSHIRE

± Cartlidge's monogram on the tile face

*'Photographic Tiles' by George Cartlidge. l to r:- Gladstone, dated 1898, 223 mm long by 148 mm wide; General Booth, 230 mm long by 150 mm wide (courtesy HCMS, DA 1977.100/1-2).*

# TORQUAY TERRA-COTTA CO.

## Hele Cross, Torquay, Devon (1875-1909)

Typical Wares: terra-cotta

### Historical Background

**The Torquay Terra-cotta Company was set up in 1875 by Dr Gillow to exploit the red clay deposits around Torquay. The clay was lighter in colour and more brittle than the clay used in the Watcombe Pottery, but the resultant wares were similar.**

Decorators at torquay included Alexander Fisher, Holland Birbeck and his son Alexander Birbeck, as well as some Italian artists. Styles were clearly influenced by the latter, and some very fine painting was accomplished by Fisher and Holland Birbeck.

The Company closed in 1909, finding it difficult to continue as a profitable business.

### Products

Fewer art wares were produced here than at Watcombe, but those that were produced consisted chiefly of vases, jugs and plaques, decorated with floral motifs. Torquay Terra-cotta were generally more decorative in their wares than at Watcombe, though there were of course many similarities between the output of the two potteries.

A similar underglaze painting technique was employed, where designs were painted directly on to the terra-cotta body, and the practice of leaving large areas of body undecorated was also similar to that of Watcombe. The characteristic large bands of turquoise enamel frequently used for decoration at Watcombe was not, however, readily adopted at Torquay Terra-cotta.

Alexander Fisher produced some fine colourful and detailed painting in enamel colours, featuring mainly birds and flowers. Holland Birbeck mostly painted realistic flower studies, which were equally detailed and colourful. White colours stood out particularly well against the smooth terra-cotta body, and convolvulus or daisies were especially striking subjects in this respect.

During the 1890's, some rare vases resembling Linthorpe products were made, characterised by a high glaze. Decoration consisted of a streaked glaze, sometimes in dual colours such as red and yellow.

Some reproductions of work by 19th Century sculptors, such as John Gibson and C B Birch were also made. Busts and figures of children and animals were produced, often in plain undecorated terra- cotta.

Some vases and jugs were also undecorated, and these are usually of simple but pleasing shapes.

**References***(see also Watcombe)*

*1) 'The Old Torquay Potteries' by D & E Lloyd Thomas, pub. Stockwell, 1978.*

*2) Catalogue of an Exhibition of Torquay Marble and Terracotta Ware at Sotheby Bearne, Torquay, 1979; pub. Sotheby Parke Bernet & Co.*

*3) 'Torquay Pottery 1870-1940'; catalogue of an Exhibition at Bearne's & Bonham's in Knightsbridge, London, August, 1986; pub. Torquay Pottery Collectors' Society.*

*4) 'Ceramics for Gentlemen of Taste: The Torquay Potteries & Their Products; article by Carol Cashmore in The Antique Dealer & Collector, August, 1986.*

*Jug, 200 mm. high.*

| Type of Ware | Production | Quality | Availability |
|---|---|---|---|
| All wares | Moderate | Poor to Very Good | Common (fine pieces scarce) |

**Marks**

| | | |
|---|---|---|
| Impressed: | TORQUAY | 1875-1909 |
| Impressed or printed: | TORQUAY<br>TERRA COTTA CO.<br>LIMITED | 1875-1890 |
| (within oval)<br>(with variations) | [TC monogram mark] | 1875-1909 |

The latter mark also appears in a circle, with the words 'Trade Mark', surrounded by the legend 'Torquay Terra Cotta Co. Limited' (c.1900-1909)

NB: Most pieces are marked but few bear an artist signature.

# UPCHURCH POTTERY 1913-c.1961

## Rainham, Kent.

Typical Wares: earthenwares

### Historical Background

**The Upchurch Pottery was established in 1913 at Rainham in Kent by Seymour Wakeley. Seymour and his brother, Sidney, were brickmakers, and operated the firm of Wakeley Brothers at the time, but the operation of the Upchurch Pottery passed quickly to William and James Baker.**

George Payne, a local antiquarian, remarked in 1915: "My friend Mr. Seymour Wakeley of Rainham has recently, at considerable cost, revived the pottery making industry upon the ancient site, selecting a spot to begin with a mile north of the parish church, and has met with marked success in the production of glazed ware suitable for table and decorative purposes. The clay used is found 2 or 3 feet below the surface of the marsh" (Archaeologia Cantiana, Vol.XXXXI,1915, p.285).

The Wakeley Brothers continued in business as agricultural merchants, operating from the old chalk pit in Seymour Road, producing oven tiles, drainpipes, flower pots and chimneys.

At the Upchurch Pottery, thrown wares were produced of the type described by George Payne. Many were designed by Edward Spencer (b.1872, d.1938), the designer and metalworker who established the Artificers' Guild with Montague Fordham in 1903. Spencer was also a member of the Arts and Crafts Exhibition Society, along with Walter Crane, Lewis Day, Charles Voysey, William Morris, Edward Burne-Jones and other worthies.

Upchurch wares were sold through retail outlets of the Artificers' Guild in London, Oxford and Cambridge until 1938, and Liberty of London, as well as locally from the Tudor Showroom in Rainham High Street. Some wares were included in the Paris Exhibition of British Decorative Arts in 1914.

From 1938, when Spencer died, the pottery became part of Rainham Potteries Ltd. and seems to have closed about 1961. Baker's son, Ted Baker, who had worked at Upchurch for a time, went on to manage Rainham Potteries Ltd. from 1938 until his retirement in 1975.

After the closure of Upchurch he operated another pottery in the group known confusingly as 'Rainham Pottery Ltd.', which specialised in commemorative wares (wall plaques and ashtrays etc. for births, weddings and anniversaries; and trophies for sports and commercial organisations). This pottery closed in 1975, the site being taken over by Otterham Caravans. (The Tudor Showroom was demolished when the caravan site was extended).

Today the existence of Wakeley Road is a remembrance of the Wakeley Brothers.

*Vase, 175 mm high, impressed mark 'UPCHURCH'.*

### Products

Wares produced at Upchurch were mostly plain pieces of simple shape. Surface decoration was kept to a minimum, and colours were mostly monochrome. A pale blue colour was used to good effect, with subtle plum-coloured splashes, but other colours utilised included pale green, buff and brown. Most colours were pastel shades.

Pieces were generally thickly potted using a red clay, and glazes were predominantly silky matt in finish. Some crystalline glazes were developed but these are scarce.

Styles were strongly influences by early Chinese or Roman forms. The Roman connection with the area was a significant influence in some of the Upchurch shapes.

Most pieces were small in size, ranging from vases and jugs to teapots, and several items were fairly crudely potted.

| Type of Ware | Production | Quality | Availability |
|---|---|---|---|
| Art wares to 1938 | Moderate | Poor to Good | Uncommon |

**Marks**

| | | |
|---|---|---|
| Incised: | Upchurch | 1913-c.1961? |
| Impressed: | UPCHURCH | 1913? - c.1961 |
| | UPCHURCH<br>SEEBY | c.1913?-c.1961? |

NB: Seeby was the name of the retail outlet at Reading, Berks.

# WATCOMBE POTTERY CO

## St. Marychurch, Torquay, Devon (1871-1901)

Typical Wares: terra-cotta

### Historical Background

**In the late 1860's, deposits of red clay were discovered around Torquay, and a firm was set up in 1869 by G Allen to exploit them. The firm was initially known as the Watcombe Terra-cotta Clay Company, and began producing pottery in 1871, assisted by skilled workmen from the Staffordshire Potteries under the direction of Charles Brock.**

By the late 1890's, six kilns were in operation, and the workforce totalled more than 100. The firm earned a high reputation, and in 1901, merged with the Aller Vale Pottery Company to form the Royal Aller Vale & Watcombe Art Potteries. Pottery was still made at Watcombe, however, until 1962.

### Products

The Watcomve Terra-cotta Clay Company at first produced terra-cotta vases, jugs and bottles, candlesticks, plaques and figures. Designs were classical, the decoration often taking the form of enamelling on the smooth red-brown terra-cotta surface.

Turquoise was a favourite enamel colour, but black and white enamels were also used. Pieces relied on simplicity of shape for effect in the true classical tradition, and surface decoration was often minimal. A common characteristic was a single band of turquoise enamel colour on the neck of vases, with either no additional decoration or hand-painted scenes on the body.

Since the terra-cotta was porous all water-holding pots had to be internally glazed. Plain or simply decorated pieces usually reveal the smooth texture of the terra-cotta body, whilst the more decorative pieces reveal the body through a transparent shiny, but thin, glaze.

During the 1870's, Samuel Kirkland modelled terra-cotta flowers and flower-baskets.

From about 1883, the pottery began to produce art wares, alongside the production of classical busts and figures of earlier styles. Surface decoration increased on the art wares, with a trend towards underglaze painting. Flowers, birds, butterflies, landscapes and seascapes were typical of the decorative subjects chosen.

During the late 1890's, Charles Brock, the manager of the pottery, invented a method of painting in oil, which began to replace the old form of enamelled decoration. He used coloured slips to paint on unburnt tiles and plaques; and a few rarely signed pieces of the oil- painted work of the artist Holland Birbeck have been found. The quality of the oil-painting was high, with detailed brushwork and often elaborate decoration. The surface of the terra-cotta was particularly suited to oil- painting, and anything with a flat enough surface, such as plaques, tiles and pilgrim bottles, was decorated to good effect.

Besides the detailed landscapes, seascapes and other motifs, some interesting geometrical patterns were produced. These and other simple decorations were often painted in black for increased effect.

The high quality painted pieces are much sought after by collectors and are consequently rarer than more general pieces.

(Refer to the chapter on Aller Vale for information on the later history of the Watcombe Pottery and its products, following the merger of the two potteries.)

| Type of Ware | Production | Quality | Availability |
|---|---|---|---|
| Early classical pieces, vases etc | Moderate | Good to Excellent | Uncommon Uncommon |
| Art wares post 1883 | Moderate | Good | Uncommon |

**Marks**

| | | |
|---|---|---|
| Impressed: | WATCOMBE TORQUAY | 1867 onwards |
| | WATCOMBE POTTERY | |
| Printed: | Consists of bird in landscape surrounded by a double circle containing the words "Watcombe South Devon". 1875-1901 | |
| Painted: | Watcombe Torquay England | slip-decorated wares of 1890's |
| Impressed: | WATCOMBE TORQUAY MADE IN ENGLAND | early 20th Century |

(The author has also noted the impressed mark 'W' and 'T' together on some wares)
± pattern or batch numbers
+ artist's mark viz:- H.B. Holland Birbeck
N.B. Few Watcombe artists signed their work. Signed pieces are therefore rare.


**References**

1) *The Victoria and Albert Museum, London has some fine enamelled vases of the classical type on display.*

2) *'English Art Pottery 1865-1915' by Malcolm Haslam, for more detailed information on the South Devon potteries.*

3) *'The Old Torquay Potteries' by D & E Lloyd Thomas, pub. Stockwell, 1978.*

4) *Catalogue of an Exhibition of Torquay Marble & Terracotta Ware at Sotheby Bearne, Torquay, 1979; pub. Sotheby Parke Bernet & Co.*

5) *'Torquay Pottery 1870-1940'; catalogue of an Exhibition at Bearne's & Bonham's in Knightsbridge, London, August, 1986; pub. Torquay Pottery Collectors' Society.*

6) *'Ceramics for Gentlemen of Taste: The Torquay Potteries & Their Products; article by Carol Cashmore; The Antique Dealer & Collector, August, 1986.*

*Jug, 215 mm high, Grecian inspired decoration, transfer printed mark in black 'WATCOMBE PORCELAIN'.*

# JOSIAH WEDGWOOD & SONS (1656 to present)

## Etruria, Staffs. (from 1769 to 1940)
## Barlaston, Staffs. (from 1940)

Typical Wares: earthenware, porcelain, moulded wares, tiles, lustres

### Historical Background

**In 1656, Thomas Wedgwood established his pottery at Burslem, exploiting the clay of the Etruria Marls. The Burslem works closed in 1744 and the site at Etruria was opened in 1769.**

Art pottery was produced from about 1880, but the most popular art pieces were made during the 20th. century, and in particular during the 1920's and early 1930's.

Wedgwood are renowned for their tablewares, but under the artistic direction of John E. Goodwin (fl. 1902-1934) a wide range of highly individual art wares were produced, including tiles.

Wedgwood were keen to fund the search for new and unusual glazes, and towards the turn of the century the chemist William Burton (at Wedgwood 1877-1892) experimented with lustre painting, producing some original blue and orange coloured glazes.

In 1893, Burton became director of the Pilkington Pottery, but his lustre painting experiments were continued by Daisy Mackeig- Jones, such that from 1914, she was able to produce some high quality art pieces which were continued throughout the 1920's until 1931. These she termed *Fairyland Lustre* and *Dragon Lustre*.

Wedgwood always had a tradition of using the designs of competent artists, and during the 1920's and 1930's several artists and designers were employed who have since become renowned for their high quality work. Artists such as Grace Barnsley were decorating wares during this period, and during the 1930's in particular original designs were created by Anna Zinkeisen, Harry Trethowan, John Skeaping, Rex Whistler, Eric Ravilious and the architect Keith Murray.

The architect Alfred Powell and his wife Louise also designed pottery for Wedgwood, from about 1905 to 1928, producing designs from their studio in London.

Wedgwood opened a special studio at Etruria in 1926 specifically for the production of pieces decorated by hand, and several young women were recruited, having trained at local art schools. The Powells regularly supplied designs for this studio, but the more talented paintresses, such as Millicent Taplin, were often allowed to implement their own designs.

In 1935, Victor Skellern became art director at Wedgwood, having been trained at Burslem School of Art by the renowned artist Gordon Forsyth. Skellern carried on the fine tradition of experiment and originality that his predecessor had introduced.

In 1940, the factory moved from Etruria to a new site at Barlaston, where it continues today, the company trading as Waterford Wedgwood (following a merger with Waterford Glass in 1986).

### Products

From about 1870 to 1900, transfer-printed tiles were produced, which included sets

*Examples of 'Fairyland Lustre' by Daisy Mackeig-Jones. l to r:- i) bowl, 70 mm high, marked 'Z11968'. ii) jar and cover, 215 mm high, marked 'Z4968'. (both with gold Portland Vase factory mark).*

such as *Robin Hood, A Midsummer Night's Dream* and *Red Riding Hood.*

About 1880, some earthenware vases were produced as art pottery, decorated in coloured slips and incorporating Japanese or Gothic designs. These early art wares are of good quality, but are scarce on the antiques market.

From about 1905, Alfred and Louise Powell were producing highly decorative pieces, using lustre glazes. Mostly simply shaped vases, jugs and bowls were decorated, using pastoral scenes and motifs with scrolled and floral borders.

From 1914, Daisy Mackeig-Jones's *Fairyland Lustres* (fantasy paintings of fairies and stars, etc.) and *Dragon Lustres.* (Chinese inspired paintings of birds, butterflies and dragons) were produced.

The lustres were executed on a porcelain body, the colours being applied over a painted surface which caused them to streak under the glaze. Occasionally gold was used over the glaze to emphasize the underlying design. Bowls large and small, saki cups, plates, vases and plaques were the main items decorated with these lustres.

The high quality and originality of the Wedgwood lustres have made them much sought after by collectors. The decoration is particularly impressive against the midnight- blue or black backgrounds, and their simple shapes enhance the spectacle immensely. Daisy Mackeig-Jones also created some ranges of nursery ware which were released form 1914 as *Noah's Ark* and *Brownies.*

In 1920, Wedgwood launched a ware named *Rhodian*, closely followed by *Persian.* Both were influenced by Near-Eastern designs and featured hand-painted decoration.

Tablewares were exhibiting more individuality of design during the 1920's and 1930's, and Wedgwood produced several ranges which reflected both the demand for creative hand- painted designs and the need for more mass-produced wares. Both art deco and modernist designs were produced, and artists such as Millicent Taplin contributed high quality designs in both styles. Her modernist *Falling Leaves* pattern in grey and green was particularly successful.

About 1927, the sculptor John Skeaping designed a series of animal sculptures which appeared in monochrome colours with a matt glaze, ranging from the renowned Wedgwood black *Basalt* ware to white, cream and pale green. Of the sculptures produced, the *Polar Bear* is particularly effective.

Modelling generally became popular at Wedgwood during the late 1920's and early 1930's, with other sculptors designing work, such as the figures produced by the American Alan Best.

During the early 1930's a series of ornamental wares entitled *Veronese* appeared. these consisted of simple shapes with simple lustre floral motifs on single coloured grounds, such as plum, green and cream. Some experiments in painting on to a tin glaze were carried out around 1935, and a few good quality gilt art deco vases were produced.

During the 1930's, Keith Murray created a range of technically precise engine-turned wares, which are now popular with collectors. Jugs, vases, bowls, trays, beer mugs and some tablewares were amongst the output of Murray's designs, and most carried a characteristically monochrome matt glaze as well as a simple shape with concentric lines or ridges.

The matt glazes were developed by Norman Wilson (at Wedgwood 1927 to 1962) and appeared in a variety of individual colours: straw, pale blue, white moonstone, pale grey, pale green, 'basalt' black, in particular. Some special glazes such as copper basalt were also used.

Murray was engaged to produce a new form of art ware that could be adapted to domestic use, and he modelled his wares on the German 'Bauhaus' style as well as on various Chinese and Korean designs. In 1933 many of these designs were exhibited at John Lewis's store in London as 'An Exhibition of New Wedgwood Shapes Designed by Keith Murray'. Favourable comments were passed at this exhibition as well as at other international exhibitions: Milan the same year, and London (1935) and Paris (1937).

Murray also helped design, in his capacity of architect, the new Wedgwood factory at Barlaston, to which the firm moved in 1940.

In 1935, Wedgwood produced a range of tea-sets called 'Farnol' in an art deco style

*Lustre bowl, 203 mm diam., by Alfred Powell. (courtesy HCMS, ACM 1946.113).*

similar to Shelley's *Mode* and *Vogue* ranges.

In 1937, Eric Ravilious created a range of *Alphabet* nursery ware, using a lithographic process of decoration, and the following year his pattern *Persephone* was produced for tablewares. Ravilious often used his graphic means of decoration to depict scenes of everyday domestic life (as seen in his *Garden* or *Garden Implements* series). Many of his designs, however, were not released until the early 1950's (his death in 1942 cutting short a promising career).

**References**

*1) 'Wedgwood Ceramics 1846-1959' by Maureen Batkin; pub. Richard Dennis, 1982.*
*2) 'Ravilious & Wedgwood' by Maureen Batkin & Robert Harling; pub. Dalrymple Press, 1986.*
*3) 'Some Glimpses of Fairyland' by M Mackeig-Jones; pub. Buten Museum of Wedgwood, 1921 (reprinted 1963).*
*4) 'The Dictionary of Wedgwood' by Robin Reilly & George Savage; pub. Antique Collectors' Club, 1980.*
*5) 'Wedgwood Fairyland Lustre, the Work of Daisy Mackeig-Jones'; catalogue by U Des Fontaines for an exhibition at Sotheby's; pub. Richard Dennis, 1978.*
*6) 'Eric Ravilious 1903- 1942:: A Re-assessment of His Life and Work'; catalogue of an exhibition at the Towner Art Gallery, Eastbourne, 1986.*
*7) 'Keith Murray' by Jill Rumsey; article in the journal of the Antique Collectors' Club, Vol. 16, No. 11, April, 1982.*

| Type of Ware | Production | Quality | Availability |
|---|---|---|---|
| Lustres (on porcelain) | Low | Very Good to Excellent | Scarce |
| Art wares (non domestic) | Moderate | Good to Very Good | Uncommon |

**Marks**

| | | |
|---|---|---|
| Impressed: | WEDGWOOD | 1929-1940 |
| Painted: | WEDGWOOD* | 1780-1940 |

+ year letter

+ artist's mark e.g. Keith Murrey (stamped in pastel blue or green)

+ 'Made in England'

* *(in gold with outline of 'Portland Vase' on many lustres and bone china)*

***Aller Vale***
*Selection of grotesques.*

***Ashtead Potters ltd***
*l to r: i) plate, 235 mm diam., decorated with concentric bands of colour, marked 'P1'. ii) three-handled thrown vase, 130 mm high, orange glaze, marked 'V36'. iii) moulded vase, 270 mm high, yellow glaze, marked 'V2'. iv) moulded muffin dish/warmer, 230 mm diam., marked 'X75'. v) moulded jug, 110 mm high, turquoise glaze, 'Liverpool' shape, marked 'J35'. vi) large moulded jug, 180 mm high, powder blue glaze, 'Brittany' shape, marked 'J16'.*

***Brannam***
*Animal group. l to r:- i) cat, 275 mm high. ii) seated dog, 125 mm high, marked 'FB'. iii) cat, 210 mm high.*

***William Moorcroft***
*A selection of early wares made at Macintyre & Co.*

***Bretby***
*Selection of wares. l to r:- i) pair of candlesticks, 224 mm high. ii) pair of vases, 320 mm high. iii) jardinere.*

***Burmantofts***

*Vase, 315 mm high, marked 'BURMANTOFT'S FAIENCE'.*

**Craven Dunhill**
*Art Pottery. l to r:- i) two-handled vase, 229 mm high, heraldic beasts decoration in red lustre on a fawn ground, white body. ii) two-handled vase, 300 mm high, classical shape, ruby lustre on white ground, white body, marked 'C.D. & Co.J' with shield, and stamped 'FORESTER'.*

**Doulton**
*Pair of vases, 147 mm high, c.1929.*

***William De Morgan***

*Group of pieces. l to r:- i) tile, 200 mm square, parrot decoration, impressed Sands End rose mark (1888-97). ii) vase, 450 mm high, fish decoration in ruby lustre by Fred Passenger, painted mark of 'De Morgan & Co' and 'FP'. iii) bowl by Fred Passenger, marked solely 'FP'. iv) vase, lion and snake lustre decoration, impressed Sands End wings mark (1888-97).*

***Elton***
*3 tygs. l to r:- i) tyg, 160 mm high, sunflower decoration with gargoyle-like heads on handles. ii) commemorative tyg in gold crackle. iii) tyg, inscribed 'Eureka' with sunflower on one panel, and tulips on two further panels (commemorating the discovery of a gold field in South Africa).*

***Farnham***
*Large charger, 480 mm diam. orange slip decoration on a brown ground, dated 1928. (courtesy HCMS, ACM 1957.64)*

***Doulton***
*A group of flambe pieces*

***Ashtead Potteries Ltd***
*'The Wembley Lion', souvenir of the British Empire Exhibition, Wembley, 1924, 102 mm high, 129 mm long. (courtesy HCMS, DA 1976.27)*

***Salopian***
*Selection of vases. l to r:- i) 'barbotine' style, 293 mm high, marked 'SALOPIAN'. ii) large vase, 280 mm high, sgraffito decoration by Hartshorne. iii) small plant pot, 78 mm high, sgraffito decoration, marked 'SALOPIAN'.*

***Doulton***

*Two Lambeth wares. l to r:- i) vase, 255 mm high, pate-sur-pate decoration with three applique unglazed white clay medallions of heads, by Eliza Simmance, marked 'Doulton Lambeth', date 1884. ii) vase, 205 mm high, early Silicon Ware on olive body, pate- sur-pate decoration with applique mosaic, marked 'Doulton Lambeth Silicon', 'OB' (olive body), c.1880.*

***Ruskin***
*Lamp-base, 200 mm high, moulded, with mottled glaze, c.1925.*

**Foley (Wileman)**
*Jardinere on stand, 1000mm high, transfer printed mark "The Foley" with monogram for Wileman & Co.*

***The Martin Brothers***
*Vases. l to r:- i) 150 mm high, signed 'R W Martin, London 9/9/1880'. ii) 240 mm high, signed 'R.W.Martin Bros, London & Southall 21/4/1883'.*

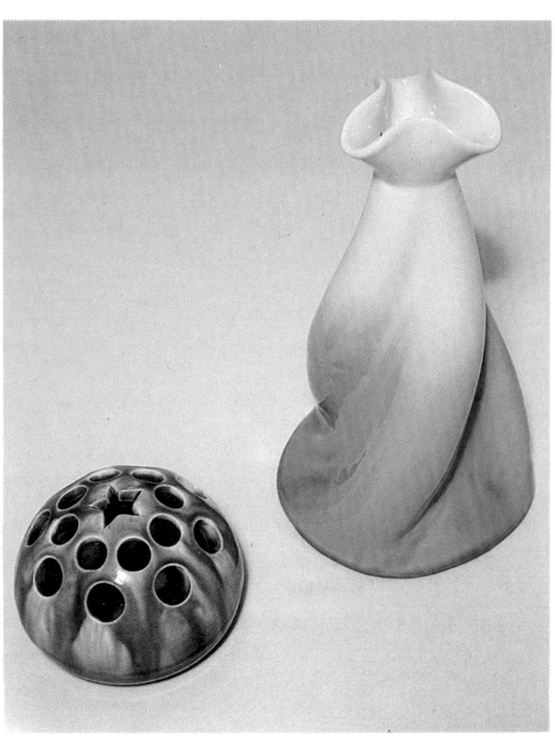

***Ault***
*Two pieces designed by Christopher Dresser. l to r:- flower holder, marked '236'; vase, 220 mm high.*

***Maw and Co.***
*Vase, 304 mm high, marked 'No 1'.*

***Rye***
*Posy vase, 94 mm high, inscribed 'Sussex Ware, Rye'.*

***Brannam***

*Vase, 245 mm high, by James Dewdney, signed 'C.H.Brannam Barum', 'JD', dated 1893.*

***Mintons***
*Jug and basin set, 360 mm high, in the 'Secessionist' style.*

*Clarice Cliff*
*Isis Vase, 25cm F & B. Isis reverse etched on base. Pattern: Orange Roof Cottage.*

## GLOSSARY OF TERMS

**BARBOTINE** - slip-wash ornamentation in low-relief.

**BISCUIT** - pottery in the undecorated state

**CELADON** - greenish feldspathic glaze, derived from iron, applied before firing.

**CLOISONNÉ** - decoration using enamel on a metal base, and secured to the pottery body.

**FAIENCE** - decorated pottery painted on a white tin-oxide ground

**FLAMBÉ** - a type of glaze, usually bright red, created by reduction at high temperatures.

**IMPASTO** - the application of colour to the raw clay.

**LUSTREWARES** - ware with a pattern painted with a high-fired 'metallic' glaze, giving a strong light reflection.

**MAJOLICA** - see 'FAIENCE'

**PARIAN WARE** - unglazed biscuit porcelain.

**PÂTE-SUR-PÂTE** - decoration by means of layers of white slip, built up into cameo-kike motifs, often against a tinted background for effect.

**SALT-GLAZE** - the application of salt as a glaze in the last stage of firing in the kiln, generally on stoneware.

**REDUCTION** - the process of firing in a kiln where oxygen has been 'reduced' in quantity. 'Flambe' colours are created in a 'reducing atmosphere'.

**SANG DE BOEUF** - a type of flambe glaze, wine-red in colour ('ox's blood')

**SGRAFFITO** - a technique of slip decoration in which a coating of slip is carefully scratched away to reveal the contrasting colour of the pottery body beneath.

**SLIP** - clay dissolved in water to the consistency of thick cream.

**TERRA-COTTA** - a fine unglazed red-bodied ware, very light in weight.

**THROWING** - the process of shaping pots on the potter's wheel.

**TUBE-LINE** - decoration with wet clay squeezed from a rubber bag to form tubular lines, rather akin to icing a cake in method.

## BIBLIOGRAPHY

This section lists publications on the subject of art pottery as covered in this book. Not all references have been consulted for the prepartion of this book, and not all are currently in print. The list is not exhaustive, but it is hoped that it will provide a sufficient cross-section of titles for the reader to seek more detailed information.
The references for a particular Pottery are also given under the chapter concerning that Pottery. Items prior to 1950 have been excluded, unless widely known.

### 1) General Period

(relating to the period covered by this book, and containing a few references to English art pottery; below is a selection of the many books available)

**Battersby, Martin** : *The Decorative Twenties*; pub. Studio Vista, 1969, (reprinted 1976) revised Philippe Garner, 1988.
**Battersby, Martin** : *The Decorative Thirties*; pub. Studio Vista, 1971, (reprinted 1976) revised Philippe Garner, 1988.
**Bayer, Patricia** : *Art Deco Souce Book - A Visual Reference to a Decorative Style 1920-40*; pub. Phaidon, 1988.
**Cameron, I. et al.** : *The Collectors' Encyclopaedia: Victoriana to Art Deco*; pub. Collin's, 1974.
**Duncan, Alastair (ed.)** : *Encyclopaedia of Art Deco*; pub. Headline, 1988.
**Garner, Philippe** : *The World of Edwardiana*; pub. Hamlyn, 1974.
**Hardy, William** : *A Guide to Art Nouveau Style*; pub. Quintet Publishing, 1986.
**Haslam, Malcolm** : *Marks & Monograms of the Modern Movement 1875-1930*; pub. Lutterworth, 1977.
**Haslam, Malcolm** : *Art Nouveau - A Buyer's Guide to the Decorative Arts of the 1900's*; pub. MacDonald Orbis, 1988.
**Hillier, Bevis** : *Art Deco - A Design Handbook*; pub. The Hubert Press Ltd., 1985.
**Klein, Dan & Margaret Bishop**: *Decorative Art 1880-1980*; pub. Phaidon, 1986.
**Klein, Dan** : *Nancy McClellan & Malcolm Haslam : In the Deco style*; pub. Thames & Hudson, 1987.
**Van De Lemme, A.** : *A Guide to Art Deco Style*; pub. Quintet Publishing, 1986.

### 2) General Pottery (mainly English ceramics)

**Barnard, J.** : *Victorian Ceramic Tiles*; pub. Studio Vista, 1972.
**Battie, David & Michael Turner**: *The Price Guide to 19th & 20th Century*
British Porcelain; pub. Antique Collectors' Club, 1975.
**Blacker, J F** : *ABC of 19th Century Ceramic Art*: pub. Stanley Paul, 1911.
**Cameron, Elisabeth** : *Encyclopaedia of Pottery & Porcelain: the 19th & 20th Centuries*; pub. Faber, 1986.
**Coysh, A W** : *British Art Pottery 1870-1940*; pub. Dabid & Charles, 1976.
**Godden, Geoffrey A** : *British Pottery, An Illustrated Guide*; pub. Barrie & Jenkins, 1974.
**Godden, Geoffrey A** : *Jewitt's Ceramic Art of Great Britain 1800-1900*; revised by G A Godden; pub. Barrie & Jenkins, 1974.
**Godden, Geoffrey A** : *Encyclopaedia of British Pottery & Porcelain Marks*; pub. Barrie & Jenkins, 1966 (revised 1979).
**Godden, Geoffrey A** : *An Illustrated Encyclopaedia of British Pottery & Porcelain*; pub. Barrie & Jenkins, 1966 (revised 1980).
**Haslam, Malcolm** : *English Art Pottery 1865-1915*; pub. Antique Collectors' Club, 1975.

**Lewis, Griselda** : *The Collector's History of English Pottery*; pub. Antique Collectors' Club, 1987.
**Lockett, Terence A** : *Collecting Victorian Tiles*; pub. Antique Collectors' Club, 1982.
**Rhead, Frederick** : *Staffordshire Pots & Potters*; pub. Hutchinson, 1906. (reprinted by E P Publishing, 1977).
**Rice, Paul** : *British Studio Ceramics*; pub. Barrie & Jenkins, 1989.
**Rose, Muriel** : *Artist Potters in England*; pub. Faber & Faber, 1955; (reprinted 1970).
**Spours, Judy** : *Art Deco Tableware (British Domestic Ceramics 1925-1939)*; pub. Ward Lock Ltd., 1988
**Thomas, E Lloyd** : *Victorian Art Pottery*; pub. Guildart, 1974.
**Wakefield, Hugh** : *Victorian Pottery*; pub. Herbert Jenkins, 1962.
**Watson, Pat** : *Collecting Art Deco Ceramics*; pub. Kevin Francis, 1989.

## 3) Specific to Artists or Potteries

**Atterbury, Paul** : *Dictionary of Minton*; pub. Antique Collectors' Club, 1988.
**Atterbury, Paul** : *Moorcroft Pottery*; pub. Richard Dennis & H Edwards, 1987.
**Atterbury, Paul** : *The Royal Doulton Story*; pub. Royal Doulton Tableware Ltd; Louise Irvine 1979.
**Batkin, Maureen & Robert Harling** : *Ravilious & Wedgwood*; pub. Dalrymple Press, 1986.
**Batkin, Maureen** : *Wedgwood Ceramics 1846-1959*; pub. Richard Dennis, 1982.
**Brannam, Peter** : *A Family Business - The Story of a Pottery*; pub. P Brannam, 1982.
**Brears, P C D** : *The Farnham Pottery*; pub. Phillimore & Co. Ltd., 1971.
**Bumpas, Bernard** : *Charlotte Rhead, Potter & Designer*; pub. Kevin Francis, 1988.
**Cashmore, Carol & Chris** : *Collard, the Honiton & Dorset Potter*; pub. Cashmore, 1983.
**Catleugh, J** : *William De Morgan Tiles*; pub. Trefoil, 1983.
**Cross, A J** : *Pilkington Royal Lancastrian Pottery & Tiles*; pub. Richard Dennis, 1980.
**Dawson, Aileen** : *Bernard Moore, Master Potter 1850-1935*; pub. Richard Dennis, 1982.
**Edgeler, Audrey** : *The Artist Potters of Barnstaple*; to be pub. Nimrod
Publications, 1989.
**Eyles, Desmond** : *The Doulton Burslem Wares*; pub. Barrie & Jenkins, 1980.
**Eyles, Desmond** : *The Doulton Lambeth Wares*; pub. Hutchinson, 1975.
**Eyles, Desmond** : *Royal Doulton 1815-1965*; pub. Hutchinson, 1965.
**Eyles, Desmond & Richard Dennis** : *Royal Doulton Figures Produced at Burslem 1890-1978*; pub. Royal Doulton Tableware, 1978.
**Eyles, Desmond, Richard Dennis** : Royal Doulton Figures produced at Staffordshire;
& Louise Irvine : pub. Royal Doulton & Richard Dennis, 1987.
**Gaunt, W & M D E, Clayton-Smith** : *William De Morgan*; pub. Studio Vista, 1971.
**Gosse, Edmund** : *Sir Henry Doulton*; (Biography ed. Desmond Eyles); pub. Hutchinson, 1970.
**Hart, Clive** : Linthorpe Art Pottery; pub. Aisling Publications, Guisborough, 1988.
**Haslam, Malcolm** : *The Martin Brothers, Potters*; pub. Richard Dennis, 1978.
**Haslam, Malcolm** : *Elton Ware - The Pottery of Sir Edmund Elton*; pub. Richard
Dennis, 1989.
**Hawkins, Jennifer** : *The Poole Potteries*; pub. Barrie & Jenkins, 1980.
**Irvine, Louise** : *Royal Doulton Figures*; pub. Richard Dennis, 1981.
**Irvine, Louise** : *Royal Doulton Series Ware*; pub. Richard Dennis. Vol. 1 1980, Vol. 2 1984, Vol.3 1986, Vol.4 1988.
**Lomax, Abraham** : *Royal Lancastrian Pottery 1900-1938*; pub. privately, 1957.
**Lukins, Jocelyn** : *Doulton Flambe Animals*; pub. privately, 1981.
**Manwaring Baines, John** : *Sussex Pottery (Rye, etc.)*; pub. Fisher Publications, 1980.
**McKeown, Jo** : *Poole Pottery - The First 100 Years*; pub. Poole Pottery, 1973.
**Mackeig-Jones, M** : *Some Glimpses of Fairyland*; pub. Buten Museum of Wedgwood, 1921, (reprinted, 1963).
**Meisel, Louis K** : *Clarice Cliff - The Bizarre Affair*; pub. Thames & Hudson, 1988.
**Niblett, Paul** : *Hand Painted Gray's Pottery*; pub. City Museum & Art Gallery, Stoke-on-Trent, 1982, 1983, new edition 1987.
**Pearson, Kevin** : *The Doulton Figure Collecters' Handbook*; pub. Kevin Francis, 1986, 1988.
**Reilly, Robin & George Savage** : *The Dictionary of Wedgwood*; pub. Antique Collectors' Club, 1980.
**Ruston, James H** : *Ruskin Pottery*; pub. Metropolitan Borough of Sandwell, 1975.
**Thomas, Lloyd D & E** : *The Old Torquay Potteries*; pub. Stockwell, 1978.
**Tyne & Wear Museums** : *Maling, a Tyneside Pottery*; pub. Tyne & Wear
County Council Museums, 1981.
**Watkins, Chris, William Harvey & Robert Senft** : *Shelley Potteries, The History*
& Production of a Staffordshire Family of Potters; pub. Barrie & Jenkins, 1980,
1986.
**Watson, Howard** : *Collecting Clarice Cliff*; pub. Kevin Francis, 1988.
**Watson, Howard** : *The Colourful World of Clarice Cliff*; pub. Kevin Francis, 1989.
**Wentworth, Peter** : *Clarice Cliff*; pub. L'Odeon, 1976 & 1981.
**Williamson Art Gallery & Museum** : *Della Robbia Pottery, Birkenhead 1894-1906,*
An Interim Report; pub. Metropolitan Borough of Wirral, c. 1974.
**Wren, Denise & Henry** : *The Oxshott Pottery*; pub. Crafts Study Centre, 1984.
**Yewman, Mick** : *The Lyle Price Guide to Doulton*; pub. Lyle Publications, 1987.

## 4) Exhibition Catalogues (major exhibitions since 1970, arranged in date order).

1970 - *Linthorpe Ware*; Exhibition at Billingham Art Gallery, Jan.
1970 - by J. Levine; pub. Teesside Museums & Art Galleries.
1971 - Catalogue of an Exhibition of Doulton Stoneware & Terracotta. 1971 - 1870-1925, Part 1; pub. Richard Dennis.
1972 - *Clarice Cliff*; catalogue of an Exhibition at the Museum & Art Gallery, Brighton.
1972 - *Christopher Dresser 1834-1904*; illustrated catalogue of an Exhibition at the Fine Arts Society, 1972; by Richard Dennis & J Jeffe.
1972 - *William De Morgan (1839-1917)*; and Exhibition at Leighton House, 1972; pub. De Morgan Foundation.
1973 - *Catalogue of Pottery by William De Morgan*; by Roger Pinkham; pub. Victoria & Albert Museum, London, 1973.
1973 - Doulton Ware & Products of Other British Potteries, the Woolley Collection including: 'Lambeth Stoneware'; by Rhoda Edwards; pub. London Borough of Lambeth, Directorate of Amenity Services, 1973.
1973 - *William Moorcroft & Walter Moorcroft (1897-1973)*; catalogue of an Exhibition at the Fine Arts Society, 1973; pub. Richard Dennis.
1975 - *Doulton Pottery from the Lambeth & Burslem Studios 1873-1939, Part 2*; pub. Richard Dennis, 1975. (see above for Part 1)
1976 - *Minton 1798-1910*; Exhibition catalogue; by E Aslin & Paul Atterbury; pub. Victoria & Albert Museum, London, 1976.
1977 - *The Art of Bernard Leach*; catalogue of a retrospective Exhibition at the Victoria & Albert Museum, 1977.

1978 - *Elegance & Utility 1924-1978*: The Work of Susie Cooper, A Tribute from Wedgwood; by Adrian Woodhouse; Exhibition at Sanderson's Showrooms, London.
1978 - *The Poole Potteries*; catalogue of an Exhibition at the Victoria & Albert Museum, London, 1978.
1978 - *Wedgwood Fairyland Lustre, the Work of Daisy Mackeig-Jones;* by U. Des Fontaines Exhibition at Sothby's; pub. Richard Dennis, 1978.
1979 - An Exhibition of Torquay Marble & Terracotta Ware at Sotheby Bearne, Torquay, 1979; catalogue pub. by Sotheby Parke Bernet & Co.
1979 - *Mabel Lucie Atwell*; catalogue of Centenary Exhibition at Brighton Museum, 1979; by A Packer.
1979 - *Christopher Dresser 1834-1904*; catalogue of an Exhibition held at Camden Arts Centre (1979) and the Dorman Museum, Middlesbrough (1980);
by Michael Collins; pub. Arkwright Trust.
1980 - *Shelley Potteries*; catalogue of an Exhibition at the Geffrye Museum, 1980.
1980 - *The Birkenhead Della Robbia Pottery, 1893-1906*; pub. Jeremy Cooper Ltd.
1981 - *Christopher Dresser, Phd.*; Catalogue by Andy Tilbrook of an Exhibition by Andy Tilbrook and Dan Klein at the Halkin Arcade, London, Autumn, 1981.
1981 - *Ruskin Pottery and the European Ceramic Revival*; catalogue of an Exhibition at Fernyhough, 1981; by I Bennet.
1982 - *Bernard Moore Master Potter 1850-1935*; Exhibition organised by Aileen Dawson & Richard Dennis, 1982. (see Bibliography (Dawson) for book published to coincide with the Exhibition).
1983 - *Burmantofts Pottery*; Exhibition at Cartwright Hall, Bradford, Nov. 1983; pub. Bradford Art Galleries & Museums; touring exhibition 1983-1988.
1984 - *Minton Tiles 1835-1935*; Exhibition catalogue; edited by D Skinner & Hans van Lemmen; pub. Stoke-on-Trent City Museum & Art Gallery, 1984.
1985 - *Hannah Barlow*; catalogue of an Exhibition at Christie's, South Kensington; by Peter Rose; pub. Richard Dennis, 1985.
1986 - *Rhead Artists & Potters 1870-1950*; catalogue of an Exhibition at the Geffrye Museum, 1986; by Bernard Bumpas; (touring exhibition).
1986 - *Eric Ravilious 1903-1942*; A Re-assissment of His Life & Work; catalogue of an Exhibition at the Towner Art Gallery, Eastbourne, 1986.
1986 - *Torquay Pottery 1870-1940*; catalogue of an Exhibition at Bearne's & Bonham's in Knightsbridge, London, August, 1986; pub. Torquay Pottery & Collectors' Soc.
1987 - *Susie Cooper Productions*; by Ann Eatwell; Exhibition at the Victoria & Albert Museum and City Museum & Art Gallery, Stoke-on-Trent; pub. V & A.
1989 - *The Designs of William de Morgan*, by Martin Greenwood; pub. Richard
Dennis & William E. Wiltshire III to coincide with an Exhibition at the Victoria
and Albert Museum, 1989.

## 5) MAGAZINES

**a) Contemporary to the period covered by this book.**

The following is a selection.

**The Art Journal (1849-1912)** (in particular 'The Art Pottery of Mr Wiliam Moorcroft' by Fred Miller, 1903)
**The Magazine of Art (1878-1902)** (in particular 'Elton Ware' by Cosmo Monkhouse, 1882)
**The Magazine of Fine Arts**
**The Potter (1893-1894)**
**The Pottery Gazette** (1875 onwards) (becoming the Pottery & Glass Trades' Review & Gazette after 1877)
**Pottery & Glass** (in particular 'Wiliam Moorcroft - A Critical Appreciation' by John Bemrose, 6/1943)
**The Studio** (1893 onwards)

**b)Magazine articles from 1970 onwards.**

The following is a selection mostly from 'The Antique Collector' (AC), 'The Antique Dealer & Collectors' Guide' (ADC) or the journal of the Antique Collectors' Club, Woodbridge, 'Antique Collecting' (ADC). The list is by no means exhaustive!

**Bartlett, John** : *Elton Ware Rediscovered*; AC; July, 1985.
**Bartlett, John** : *Elton Ware*; Bristol Illustrated; November, 1986.
**Bartlett, John** : *Elton Ware - The Genius of Sir Edmund Elton, Potter-Baronet*; ACC; Vol. 21, No.9, February 1987.
**Bracegirdle, Cyril** : *Linthorpe, the Forgotten Pottery*; Country Life; 1971.
**Bumpas, Bernard** : *Cheerful Charlotte Rhead*; ADC; August, 1988.
**Bumpas, Bernard** : *Pottery Designed by Charlotte Rhead*; AC; January, 1983.
**Bumpas, Bernard** : *Tube-Line Variations*; AC; December, 1985.
**Cashmore, Carol** : *Ceramics for Gentlemen of Taste: The Torquay Potteries & Their Products*; ADC; August, 1986.
**Cashmore, Carol** : *Honiton - A Neglected Pottery*; ADC; May, 1987.
**Cross, A J** : *Pilkington's Royal Lancastrian Pottery 1904-57*; ADC; September, 1973.
**Crossingham-Gower :** *Susie Cooper - Pride of the Potteries*; Art & Antiques, April Graham 12, 1975.
**Crossingham-Gower** : *The Potters of Poole*; Art & Antiques; March 22, 1975.
**Eatwell, A** : *A Bold Experiment in Tableware Design (1934 Harrods' Exhibition)*; ACC; November, 1984, Vol.19, No.6.
**Elton, Julia** : *Eltonware at Clevedon Court*; National Trust Magazine; 1980.
**Fletcher, Neil** : *Sixty Glorious Years - The Work of Susie Cooper, OBE*; ACC; Vol. 19, No.5, October, 1984.
**James, Susan** : *Barum Ware - The Work of C H Brannam (1855-1937)*; AC; August, 1973.
**Knowles, Eric** : *Photographic Portrait Tiles (George Cartlidge, Sherwin & Cotton)*; AC; August, 1977.
**McDonald, C Haig** : *Excellent in its Simplicity (Susie Cooper)*; AC; July, 1987.
**Mortimer, Tony L** : *The Royal Lancastrian Pottery*; ACC; Vol. 20, No. 4, September, 1985.
**Mutler, Grant** : *Minton Secessionist Ware*; The Connoisseur; August, 1980.
**Peake, Graham** : *In the Advance Spirit (Susie Cooper)*; ADC; July, 1987.
**Pinkham, Roger** : *A Tale of Three Potteries (Linthorpe, Ault, Bretby)*; AC; September 1977.
**Ruck, Pamela** : *A Victorian Squire & His Eccentric Pottery (Elton)*; Art & Antiques March 27, 1976.
**Rumsey, Jill** : *Keith Murray*; ACC; Vol. 16, No.11, April, 1982.
**Snodin, Su** : *Susie Cooper, Diverse Designer*; AC; August, 1982.
**Stirling E** : *Carlton Ware: Naturalistic Patterns of the 1930's and 1940's*; ACC; May, 1984, Vol. 19, No. 1
**Summerfield, Angela** : *The Martin Brothers*; AC; November, 1987.
**Thornton, Lynne** : *Pilkington's Royal Lancastrian Lustre Pottery*; The Connoisseur; May, 1970.
**Wade, Hilary** : *Christopher Dresser & The Linthorpe Potteries*; AC; February, 1984.
**Watson, Pat** : *Commercial Courage (Clarice Cliff)*; ADC; August, 1988.
**Winstone, Victor** : *As Fresh as 50 Years Ago (Susie Cooper)*; Art & Antiques, June 19, 1978.

# INDEX

# Kevin Francis Publishing

**Our latest titles for 1989/90:**

**The Colourfuful World of Clarice Cliff £19.95**

**Charlotte Rhead £9.95**

**Collecting Clarice Cliff £12.95**

**Collecting Art Deco Ceramics £17.95**

**English Decorative Ceramics £17.95**

Enrol in our book club for the latest in developments in the ceramics market,
trends, new books, items for sale etc.
Write to: **Kevin Francis Pubishing, FREEPOST, LONDON SE22 9BR.**

**For one of the biggest ranges of Decorative Ceramics in the country in a unique and friendly atmosphere. See you soon.**

TELEPHONE 01-262 1576
30 CHURCH STREET · MARYLEBONE · LONDON NW8
VAT NO. 511 1164 09

THE AGE OF JAZZ LINGERS ON
1920's/30's CERAMICS BY CLARICE CLIFF, SUSIE COOPER, CHARLOTTE RHEAD AND OTHERS. ART DECO FURNITURE, MIRRORS, CHROME AND LIGHTING BOUGHT AND SOLD
MUIR HEWITT, HALIFAX ANTIQUES CENTRE (NOT THE PIECE HALL), QUEENS ROAD MILLS, QUEENS ROAD/GIBBET STREET, HALIFAX HX1 4LR
OPEN TUESDAY—SATURDAY 10 am - 5 pm TEL 0422 366657 — EVENINGS 0274 882051
MEDIUM WAVES 200/550 METRES
LONG WAVES 900/2000 METRES